W9-BNM-710

life is not fair...

*and everything else
they forgot to teach
you in school*

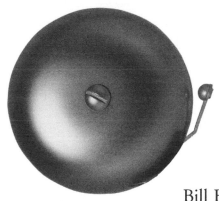

Bill Bernard

SOURCEBOOKS, INC.®
NAPERVILLE, ILLINOIS

Published by Sourcebooks, Inc.
P.O. Box 4410, Naperville, Illinois 60567-4410
(630) 961-3900
FAX: (630) 961-2168
www.sourcebooks.com

Bernard, Bill.
Life is not fair... and everything else they forgot to teach you in school / Bill Bernard.
    p. cm.
  ISBN 1-4022-0279-2 (alk. paper)
1. Teenagers--Life skills guides. 2. Adolescent psychology. I. Title.
HQ796.B424 2004
646.7'00835--dc22

                                    2004012236

                        Printed and bound in Canada
                    WC   10 9 8 7 6 5 4 3 2 1

If you don't know where you're going,
any road will take you there.

—Ancient Jewish Proverb

TABLE OF CONTENTS

author to reader

If you are reading this, you are probably really, really bummed. This is so stupid! What could you possibly learn about life from a stupid book? Your parents don't have a clue, and neither does the yahoo who wrote this. Nobody really understands. Things are just fine. *If you would all just leave me alone!* Is this what's going through your head right now, or are you just wondering who logged on to IM?

This book is written for teenagers and their parents. It's a book about the "Facts of Life." These are not the Facts of Life you have always heard about, the sex and pregnancy stuff. This is about the *real* Facts of Life. It's about how the world really works, and how you can get ahead. It's a book about thinking. It's a little about "what" to think and mostly about "how" to think. It's kind of like an Instruction Manual for life—you know, number one, take all the pieces out of the box and check to see that you have all the right parts.

So, the world is going to happen to you whether you like it or not. How you "deal" with the world is going to have a really big impact on how it "deals" with you (there's a lot of give and take here). It's simple stuff! You may think you have a pretty good handle on how the world works (people, relationships, money, sex), but you don't. Trust me, most people don't. I am going to give you a chance to see these things from a completely different perspective and whether you agree with me or not, simply going through the process should be rather illuminating. It's like the joke about the drunk leaning against the lamp post. Is he using it for illumination or support? You should use this book for both. Coming to grips with the world and how it works will allow you to make more money, have better friends, form better relationships, and simply have more fun. Who wouldn't want to do this? So, here it is. Take it or leave it. At the very least, you might find a new way of looking at how things work and how you can make them work for you.

The point is not to simply read this stuff and say: Oh, that's interesting. You should really *think* about these things and figure out how *you* feel about them. You're the one that has to live with your life and you're the only one who's going to be stuck with it. It's all about how you're going to end up.

How you end up will a have a whole lot to do with how well you think. The better you learn to think, the fewer mistakes you'll make—and with fewer mistakes, you'll end up much better off! Using your brain will help you avoid many mistakes, but you'll never avoid all of them. Expect to make them and learn from them. Make sure you're thinking. A little tip here; don't let your mistakes cause you to make further mistakes. This is called "compounding your errors" and inevitably ends in disaster. You can get so caught up in trying to fix a mistake that you make more and more, digging a very deep hole. When you make a mistake, accept it and think how you'll keep it from happening again. This is the best thing you can use your brain for.

I remember once seeing an ad in a magazine. It showed an artists' pallet smeared with colorful oil paints and some brushes. It said, "knowing what it is doesn't tell you how to use it!" I think we are all in same boat with our thinking and our lives. We know what life is—it happens suddenly every morning when we wake up—but no one has ever spent much time telling us how to best *use* our lives, our time on this planet. With this in mind, I set out to define the way I've learned to think about thinking and about life, the connections between what you do and what you get, and that's ultimately what everything is all about.

Before we go on though, we're going to have to cover a few basics.

THE WORLD

When I talk about the world, I am not talking about the planet or the globe. I'm talking about the place where you live and work and go to school and have fun. I am talking about whatever "world" you live in and all the stuff that goes on within it—all the stuff that happens to you or that you can expect to happen to you. I'm also talking about your World View. A "World View" is the sum of everything you *choose* to accept as truth, the Facts of Life about the world you live in. It's all about your beliefs (not the religious kind). You might believe that the Mets are a crappy baseball team, that younger kids are stupid, that your dad is unreasonable, and Jupiter is the most distant planet from the sun. There are a whole lot of things we "believe." Some of the stuff we believe is the absolute truth, and some of it is a bunch of crap. How you sort it all out is your World View, the sum of all the Facts of Life you've *chosen* to believe. "Choice" is the key word here.

Let's imagine a beautiful meadow in the forest somewhere—mountains in the distance, trees, a stream, elk and rabbits and birds and butterflies, the whole shooting match. Now let's imagine that someone has built a long, narrow cement bunker in the middle of this beautiful meadow. This bunker has a cement roof and four cement walls, with only one small window way down at the far end. Imagine you're standing inside the bunker at the other end, looking out the small window.

This is your world when you are born. You only see this tiny bit of the real world outside the bunker. Every week and month and year you are alive, you get a little closer to this window, and you can see a little more of the real world outside. As a teenager, you are about a quarter of the way to the window, and the world looks a lot bigger than it did when you started, so you think you know quite a bit about it. You can now tell that that bushy green thing is really a tree, and that the sound is coming from a stream, but you're still only seeing a small amount of what's *really* out there. This is the way it is with your World View, the things you believe. The more you see, the more things will make sense. The more you see, the more your beliefs will change. Hell, you used to believe in Santa Claus! So, if someone knocked on the door of your bunker and came inside to tell you about the "outside," I would hope you would be pretty interested. That's what this book is about: It's about stuff "outside" your existing experience—outside your bunker.

The Facts of Life in this book are important because they form the basis for how you see the world and your place in it. The way most people learn about the Facts of Life is through direct experience. Stuff happens to you, you hear stories, people tell you things. We usually pick out things that agree with what we already believe and ignore the things that don't (the Mets *are* a crappy baseball team, and Jupiter *isn't* the furthest planet from the Sun). Sometimes, if you believe something that's wrong it causes you to ignore something that's right. This has a double effect in that you are not only believing a wrong thing, but not but not believing a right thing. This screws up your World View and keeps you from really understanding how life works. So, your choices here (what you believe about the world and what you don't) form the basis for how you make decisions, what decisions you make, and generally how you go about living your life. These beliefs are going to be with you for a long, long time, so it's a pretty good idea to stop for a minute and really examine *why* you think certain things are the way they are.

Being a teenager is pretty miserable, always has been. George Bernard Shaw was one of England's poet laureates. When he was an old man, he was asked if he wouldn't "love" to be eighteen again. He replied that this was the most idiotic thing he had ever heard. Of course he wouldn't want to be eighteen again. It was horrible the first time!

Part of what makes the teenage years so awful is physical. You have a pretty adult body that's being controlled by a brain that just isn't working very well yet. Your brain doesn't work very well because you don't have enough experience to draw on. It's like having a nifty new computer and no programs to run on it! Experience is how you get programmed. You haven't seen enough of what's outside that window in your bunker. You hate this, but deep down you know it's true. You simply haven't been around long enough. Accept it—it's OK.

Kurt Vonnegut, a writer, gave a commencement address to some prestigious Eastern college, and was asked what he thought should be done about some issue, with his lifetime of human observations as a very successful author. He replied,

"How the hell should I know, I just got here!" He meant that even with his sixty-plus years on this planet, he still didn't feel he had enough "experience" to answer the question.

Another reason it's miserable to be a teenager is because you are just brimming over with potential, but you really don't know how to do very much yet. You have the potential to do anything, or so everybody keeps telling you, but you don't have a clue as to what it should be. Potential is a huge obligation that we never ask for. You are really nervous about screwing it up, so you've decided to pretend that you don't care. Get over it—you do and should care!

All of this misery, anguish, and conflict can be eliminated a lot faster than you could imagine. All of your fears, anxieties, nervousness, and insecurity can vanish if you take a little time to think about your World View and the Facts of Life you have chosen (or been forced) to believe. *The easiest and quickest way to start feeling better about yourself, and better about your place in the world, is to simply start looking at the world from a different perspective.*

I am *not* saying that I have all the answers, or that this book provides all the "right" ways to see the world, or even the "best" way to see the world. Everyone has to eventually figure all this stuff out on their own. The point is, you need to start figuring this stuff out fairly quickly. Decisions you are going to be making in the next couple of years will have a big impact on the life you end up living. It's like aiming a rifle. Moving the barrel just a little bit, where the bullet starts, has a big impact on where the bullet it ends up! You should go into this period of your life with a good understanding of what you *really* believe. All I hope to do here is to just have a few light bulbs go off, to have you start thinking about some really important issues. This stuff is just as important as the stuff you are supposedly learning in school— Algebra, U.S. History, or the chemical composition of methane. You should put some decent time and effort into *this* stuff too!

THINKING

Like everything else you can learn, thinking is a skill—and like any skill, you will do much better with a little instruction and practice. Nothing you can ever do will be as important as learning how to think a little better. It will serve you well. You should be using this skill every minute of every day. Right now, as you are reading this, hopefully you are thinking. You're probably thinking that your thinking is OK, and that this is stupid and just a waste of your time. Perfect! Be critical, be suspicious, don't accept anything at face value—examine it, understand it, and *choose* to agree or disagree. That's how thinking works. You are the master of your destiny. You choose what to believe and what not to believe.

So, how do you teach someone to think? Unfortunately you can't! This is something you have to learn on your own. Some things in life need to be learned—but can't really be taught. Catching a baseball can't really be taught. Someone can demonstrate techniques and the principles, but you have to actually catch the ball yourself to really learn how to do it. When you're teaching kids to play catch, you don't scream and yell the first time they drop the ball. You do it again and again until they get it. With thinking though, we have a tendency to be very critical the first time someone drops the ball. If you're the one dropping the ball, or the one being critical, stop it! Try it again and again until you get it right.

❊ ❊ ❊

The first lesson about thinking is that you can actually *choose* both *what* you think about and *how* you think about it. Thinking doesn't have to be like some scrap of paper blown around by the wind. Your thinking wanders around only if you let it, but you can also learn how to exercise some control over your own thoughts.

Everybody mostly thinks about three things. They think about things that have happened (the past), things that are happening (the present) and things that might happen (the future). Thinking about the future is the most fun and we probably spend a lot of our time doing this. This is the great "What if…" kind of thinking. Life teaches us early on that this is bad; someone has invariably said, "Stop daydreaming!" Truth is, this is the best kind of thinking you can do, but we usually don't take it to its logical conclusion. We think, "Wouldn't it be great if…" We come up with elaborate fantasies, complicated situations where we are the hero or heroine, and then we stop! If we really liked what we were thinking about, we should then try to figure out how to get there. This is called "Forward Thinking." How can I make something happen?

If you think that it would be really cool to be president of the United States (yeeesh!), you could do that. It would be really hard, but you would have a chance if you went to an Ivy League college, got a degree in law, started by running for local political offices, became a big shot in your political party, moved up the ladder, and so on and so on. The odds may be pretty low, but every president (except for the early guys) started out as a kid who thought about being president. Basically, your odds are one in three hundred million. One out of the roughly three hundred million people in the United States becomes the president, and not a single one of them ended up there by accident.

Forward Thinking is to always take the next step in the "wouldn't it be cool" process and to think about how you would get from point A to point B. If it seems like it would be worth the trouble, then go for it. If you think it's way too much effort, then think about something else. Think about the logical connection between what you want and what you have to do to get it. If you don't want to do the work, then stop complaining. Don't use "sour grapes" as an excuse for being lazy. Everything requires work. This is the hardest lesson to get. Work produces stuff. If you want stuff, you've got to do the work! You can do almost anything. This is a Fact of Life. Believe it—it just takes *work*. (Don't get too carried away though, some things are just stupid. If you are a fifty-year-old woman, the odds are pretty small that you have any chance of ever being a Super Bowl quarterback.) *Practice thinking about connections. If I do "that," "this" is likely to happen. If I want "this" to happen, I will have the best chances of achieving it if I do "that."* You probably already do some of this, but you need to stick with it, do it more often, and do it better. The "doing" is the big word here. It's like playing catch.

COUNTER INTUITION

("Counter Intuition" is usually spelled as one word, but it is much more dramatic this way!)

Counter Intuition is defined by the *Microsoft Encarta College Dictionary* as "not in accordance with what would naturally be assumed or expected." In other words, few things in life are as they first appear to be. Really keeping this notion up front in your mind will help you be more patient in your rush to be right and to "know" any answer. This is the "know" as in "Yeah, yeah, yeah, I know, I know." You probably don't. Learning to accept this simple fact will save you tons of grief! Everyone wants to be right. Everyone wants to know. We are all taught early on to be quick with an answer, quick to be the one who "knows."

Way back when, sitting in a classroom of thirty kids, we all remember wanting to be the first one with the answer, the first one to be called on. If we were shy, didn't know the answer, or were afraid of being wrong, we would make fun of the "teacher's pet" and "the nerd." This usually happens around first or second grade when we are taught two very destructive and "wrong" lessons about life. (These "wrong" lessons tend to make us very poor thinkers.) The first is the lesson that the kid with the quickest answer is the smartest. The second is the lesson that it is much "cooler" to be stupid, to not be the "nerd." No one makes fun of you if you keep your mouth shut. We learn from this that if we want to appear smart, we try to rush into the quickest (and usually wrong) answers, and if we want to be cool we try to appear stupid. The worst case is when one combines both of these beliefs and tries to be both smart and cool at the same time (usually being quick with a stupid answer, being a "smart ass"). *This is a common teenage mistake, and a bad strategy for life.* Trying to be "smart" and "cool" results in all those stupid arguments that end up with equally stupid childhood bets: "Oh yeah, well you have to walk around all day in your underwear if New York *is* a city and *not* a state!" You know what I'm talking about, and you know how ridiculous you felt when you found out how wrong you were! Just seeing this fact in black and white should make you see the errors in this kind of thinking—the smart/cool conundrum.

The right thing and the best thing is not to be the quickest to judgment, the quickest to answer. The right thing is that it's very cool to be smart, and no matter how smart you think you are, you always have something more you can learn. The right thing is that usually the smartest thing anyone can ever say is simply, "I don't know." Perhaps the most important thing you can learn in life is to admit when you are wrong. These simple, "real" facts (it's cool to be smart, being smart is not always quick, and it's stupid to try to be so cool) are *counterintuitive* based on what we are taught in first and second grades.

DIRECTIONS

Before we get started, you will need to get several things together in order to use this book.

1. something of value
2. a yardstick with a hole in one end
3. a foam-backed poster board
4. a thumb tack
5. a pencil
6. a watch or clock
7. a calculator

This book is divided into ten sections, and each section is put together like a unit in a college class. The introduction is not a section; it is here only to let you know what this is all about—some general concepts that will help as you go along. I suggest that you go through each section with your parents. The more the merrier. I have written this to be read out loud and I suggest you take turns reading it this way. I hope it is neither too long or too boring. Each section should only take about thirty minutes to read, and about thirty minutes to discuss. At the end of each section there is a summary of the key points and several questions. These questions should help you with the discussion. Take turns answering these questions and discuss your answers. There is no right or wrong. It's all about your thinking. You should try to do one section a night for ten consecutive nights. This may be hard to do, but the discipline is a good thing. Learning how to think is hard work.

So, as you start this process, always keep in the back of your mind that I'm not really talking about *what* to think, but *how* to think. I'll use the Facts of Life as an outline. Thinking is a skill that needs to be practiced. You get it wrong a lot when you first start, so give yourself a break. Think about things in a counterintuitive manner. Think that things are never really how they appear at first. Be critical and try to see how some things can teach us the totally wrong lessons about how life really is. Think about the "real" rules to life. Learn to control your thinking, and learn to always take the next step in the process. Think forward. Have a plan. Understand and act accordingly.

Section One

there are no "free" lunches!

(How to Get People to Leave You Alone)

OK, here we go. There's a lot of stuff in this book, and some parts may be more helpful to you than other parts. USE THIS BOOK! Earmark (fold over) pages that are important to you. Make notes, underline things, get a highlighter. Go back and reread the stuff that matters to you.

In this section, you will learn how to get anyone to leave you alone by understanding that there is no such thing as a free lunch! Knowing what this *really* means, *really* getting it and keeping it in mind, will allow you to keep everyone off your back forever. This includes your parents, your siblings, your teachers, your significant others, your bosses—guaranteed!

There's a catch though. You have to really think about it, really get into the "implications," to really get it.

"There is no such thing as a free lunch," is a business phrase, but it is the first step in understanding how the world works. This is the world you are going to have to live in, whether you're in business or not, whether you like it or not. It's a good place to start because it's about dealing with other people, and this is one of the most important things you're going to do throughout your life. It's about seeing interactions between people as "transactions."

"UNFAIRNESS"

Before I go on, I have to mention that many of the things I write about in this book are things that you are going to think are totally unfair. Part of becoming an adult is understanding the general "unfairness" of the world and getting over it.

Let's take a look at "fairness" so that we can be done with it once and for all. Kids play a lot of games. You grow up with board games and card games and sports. All these games have rules, and if everyone knows the rules it's totally fair. Luck or skill or both determine the outcome. In soccer, being offside is being offside—it's a rule. Does anyone ever go on and on about whether it's fair or not? No. You might argue about whether you really were offside or not, but I bet you have never heard anyone argue about whether or not the *rule* was fair. Life is kind of the same, but here we complain about the rules because we don't really understand them. The games kids play teach them to expect that the whole world works the way games do. It doesn't! (Remember Counter Intuition.) In fact, the real world works exactly the opposite of this. The whole world is *based* on "unfairness," and this is one of the first "real" rules you need to learn. Games are supposed to be fair, but life isn't.

People, companies, groups, countries, families—almost everyone goes to great lengths to make sure things are *not* fair. They all want to have an advantage. They all want the "rules" to favor them so that they don't have to rely so much on skill or luck. Trust me, this is the way it is. Laws, taxes, international treaties, and contracts are all designed to be as unfair as they possibly can, to give the advantage to one group or another. Most divorce laws greatly favor the woman. This is not fair. Rich people (who have more influence on laws because of their money) pay far less in taxes (a smaller percentage) than poor people. This is not fair. A dress that is made in Costa Rica sells for $75 in a store in California. The store makes about $35, the distributor makes about $20, the importer makes about $10, the manufacturer makes about $9 and the woman who actually sewed the dress makes $1. This is not fair. This is the "real" world, so let's get over the whole "fairness" thing for right now and just concentrate on how we should be thinking, and how life *really* works.

RULES SUCK

Understanding the "real" rules, like the "unfairness" rule, will allow you to *make more money, be happier, and have more fun!* If you don't know these "real" rules, or if you think about them the wrong way, you are at a decided disadvantage in life. The problem with the "real" rules is that most people hardly ever talk about them, and even when they do, they talk about the way things should be, or the way they would like them to be, and not the way they really are.

There are really "big" rules. These say that you shouldn't kill someone (the Ten Commandments kind of rules). These really big rules have become laws and are about making whole societies work. I will not really deal with these kind of rules because, for the most part, we get them. These are the rules that, when broken, send people to prison.

There are medium-sized rules. These are the "do unto others as you would have them do unto you" types of rules. These are the ones I am most interested in because they have to do with how an individual gets along in life. They are not about societies, but about people. These are the rules where there is the most confusion. There's confusion because the people who are always talking about these rules are also the ones who seldom follow them. The "Golden Rule" ("Do unto others as you would have them do unto you") or the "Karma" rule ("Whatever you do will come back at you") are familiar to us all and they make considerable sense when you say them out loud. The problem with these rules is that they are about the way we would "like" things to be, but not the way they really are. We hear about these rules, but we don't see them working. We see the devout Christian telling nasty jokes, "There's these three gay guys and a hooker…" (no Golden

Rule here). We see the self-possessed, greedy businessman making millions off of other people's suffering (no Karma rule here). We're confused because "real" life doesn't follow these kinds of medium-sized rules. Real life follows rules that are not so nice and pretty. These real rules are not friendly, they're not fair, they just are what they are. Get used to it. (Maybe this is why nobody really talks about them very much.)

Remember that all rules, although we usually hate them, are very important! You can't play any game, whether it's baseball, monopoly, or soccer, without knowing the rules. You can try, but it's never very much fun. It wasn't fun when you didn't know the rules to some game you tried to play, and it was even worse when you cheated. Worse yet happens when everyone "thinks" they know the rules and they don't. It's always stupid, boring, and full of arguments. We've all been there ("I'm not out, you can't do that, it's not fair!").

This book is about the "secret" rules to life—the way things really are and how they can make a big difference in whether you're successful or not. It's not that everything you know is wrong (as the old comedy routine once started), but that even though you may be on the right track, you need to also be *thinking* about it the right way. This is the first step in rethinking your thinking process. Don't be so sure of yourself; things are not always how they seem to be. Going through this short book with your parents can help you understand the real, gritty, nasty world a little better. This place changes a lot. Ask any politician!

A Little Rule

My mom let my brother's friend Steve come over one night and spend the night. My mom came into my room and said, "Now tell me if there's anything that's happening, like if they are going to do anything bad or anything," and I said "OK," and then later I went to sleep. Ben, my brother, comes and wakes me up, and he's really scared, and then he says, "I snuck two girls in— don't tell Mom." So I was like, "OK?" because I always have to cover for Ben. So then my mom comes in and she says, "Do you hear girls in there?" I say, "No, I think that's just Steve laughing." My mom tells me she's going to go get her robe and check to see if any girls are in there. So, when she went to go do that, I ran to Ben's room and said that Mom's coming, and Ben had a very surprised look on his face. So then my mom comes by, and I was really scared that she might catch me and be disappointed that I didn't listen to her, or that I was trying to cover for Ben, whatever! I was really scared. I was like shaking and stuff. My mom goes in and Ben was hiding the girls in his closet. She's like, "Are there any girls in there?" and he's like, "No, it's just me and Steve," and she's like, "Are you sure?" and he's like, "Yeah, I think I know what's in my room." Then she goes away, and says goodnight to me again, and I'm like still shaking and so, yeah, the girls spent the night. Ben broke the rules about having no girls in his room. Steve and him claimed to leave at 5:30 in the morning to go surfing, and they did, but also another reason they left at 5:30 is so they could sneak the girls out and take them home. So, Ben broke a rule he knew about, and because he did this, I had to break a rule I knew about. The thing is, my mom broke a rule too, probably one she didn't know about. I mean, why is she asking me to snitch on Ben? I'm not his boss, and even if he does something wrong, why do I have to be in the middle? I think you really have to stay out of the middle of things.

Hannah—13

Now that we have the "unfairness" thing and the need for rules out of the way, we can get on with it. In the introduction I listed Something of Value as one of the supplies you need. You and your parents should agree on what this Something of Value is—something that you will get if you read this book with them. It could be money, something you want, a favor, or whatever, but you should agree that if you read this book with them and talk about the questions in each section, you will receive what you have chosen. Is that fair? Something of Value for about ten hours of reading and talking?

Even though it's pretty easy work, you will still have to do *some* work for the Something of Value. There is no such thing as a free lunch! You don't have to agree with what's here. The whole point is just to learn how to think about it a little bit better. Prove that you're not just blowing this off, and you get the dough. Is that fair? If so, you know the rules of this transaction, and you should be starting to get the free lunch thing. You have to put in ten hours of time to get Something of Value (nothing free here), and your parents have to cough-up Something of Value to get you to read this book with them (nothing free there).

GIMME, GIMME, GIMME

So how do you get people to leave you alone? You do that by understanding why the free lunch is never free. It's not free because it *always* comes with an obligation. This obligation is always different, but you have to know that it's *always* there. Every time someone does something for you, even the littlest thing, you owe them—whether you like it or not. This is how life works. If you don't pay up, you remain in debt, and no one likes bad debt or "moochers."

You may say, "Oh, well I didn't ask for that, and if I didn't ask for it, I shouldn't have to pay." Wrong! You pay for a lot of things you never asked for. You didn't ask to go to school, but you pay six hours of your life, five days a week because you have to! You didn't ask to have someone smash into your mother's car while you were driving, but someone has to pay, and it's going to be you or your parents if the other guy has no insurance. If someone walked up to you on the street and handed you a $100 bill out of the blue, you would probably ask if there was a catch, something you had to do for the $100. You would naturally expect some sort of obligation. In much of your life, you *expect* these obligations to come with things given to you, but it's only when you don't "want" to pay up that you start going on and on about how it isn't "fair." *The Life Lesson here is that you don't get to pick and choose. If you have an obligation, whether you wanted it or not, you owe!*

Your parents think that you owe them a lot, all that money and all the time and effort that it took to raise you to where you are today. You don't think you owe them anything. You never asked to be born, or asked to be raised—those things are just expected, right? You hate this because nobody, and I mean *nobody*, likes to be in this kind of debt, especially if you see that debt as extraordinary or unfair. This is one of the biggest reasons you and your parents don't get along, and perhaps why you are reading this right now. It all comes down to a misunderstanding of the fact that everyone owes everyone a whole lot, that we are somehow "entitled," that we should be able to have certain things without owing anything.

IT'S ALL ABOUT ME!

Entitlement is a good word. It means having a sense that you are owed something just because you exist. You look at your house, the food on the table, a comfortable bed, etc. and feel that you are owed this stuff for being a kid, for not "asking" to be born. You feel your parents and the world in general owes you something just because you showed up. A lot of people waste their whole lives bitching about everything they think they are owed. This is very wrong too! The right way to "think" about obligations, the right way to think about what you owe, is that you have to pay up! *You should always respect the debts you owe to others, but never expect anything being owed to you.* Sounds kind of "unfair," but that's the way it is in the real world. Expect to get stiffed, but never stiff anyone yourself!

Your parents might "owe" the mortgage on your house or the note on their car, but they are not "entitled" to them simply because they're nice people, or good parents, or honorable. If they miss a payment, the house or the car gets yanked. Everyone who ever saw the movie *Repo Man* understands this. What we don't usually get is that all the "intangible" debts we owe (favors, obligations, expectations) don't have such clear-cut rules. A friend may think you owe them a favor, but you think *they* owe *you* the favor. If this goes on too long, or doesn't get resolved, the friendship usually ends, but we don't really look at this the same way as getting our car repossessed. You should! The friendship was "repossessed" for lack of payment. Get used to thinking that *you* are going to have to pay all *your* debts, but that for the most part, no one else is ever going to want to pay *theirs* to you!

Kids feel entitled. They feel that their parents' stuff (and position in life) also belongs to them. It doesn't. Everyone starts out in life exactly the same. Everyone starts with nothing. In an episode of *The Cosby Show*, Bill Cosby's son says to his dad that he should have something he wants because "We're rich!" Cosby explains, "No son, your Mom and I are rich, you are not rich. You have nothing!" This is a good way to start thinking about entitlement. As a teenager, almost everything you have has been given to you. You probably haven't really "earned" very much. This is OK, but think about this stuff as "gifts." This is a huge step in growing up—appreciating all the gifts and advantages you have received! Seeing whatever it is you've been given as a wonderful present. If you think about it, you should see how much this changes your attitude. Say two kids are each given a car to drive. The kid who thinks he is entitled to the car (after all, he does have a license now) appreciates the car, but usually thinks he is entitled to even more (after all, it's not as nice as his parents' cars). The kid who does not feel entitled sees the car as a huge gift for which he "owes" a lot of appreciation. He is thrilled and thinks about what a good deal he got every time he gets inside. Who do you think is happier? What's the better attitude?

TRANSACTION SATISFACTION

As I said, the free-lunch phrase comes from business because there are a lot of lunch meetings in business. Someone is always selling and someone is always being sold to—always, each and every time. Sometimes, it's very clear—this guy is trying to sell that guy a forklift for $30,000. Most times it's not so clear—this guy is selling how cool he is to that girl so that she will go out with him. Often it's not clear at all—this guy is selling his thoughts to that guy so the other guy will simply agree with him and make him feel better about himself. Most people think of "selling" and "being sold to" as a seedy sort of bad thing. This is another idea we have been taught early on in life that is wrong (think of the phrases "He was sold down the river," "He was sold a bill of goods," "Why, he'd sell his own grandmother!").

I can see how this spin on selling is supported by those who get the fact that selling is a good thing. This spin keeps the competition down, keeps people from wanting their well-paying jobs! People need a lot of stuff and sellers help them get it. Think about how much stuff you need or want to buy—somebody's got to sell it to you or you can't get it. So forget about the selling spin and just think of "transactions." It's funny how there is no spin attached to this word. This is also a big Life Lesson in the real world: *Whenever two or more people are together, there is always a transaction taking place.*

There is not only a transaction always taking place, but there are "rules" to the transaction too! The seller almost always buys the lunch, and the buyer has the obligation to listen until the food is gone, or in some cases, even the obligation to buy what's being sold. So, if you are selling, you have to pay for lunch! If you're buying, you have to listen! The listening is the price you have to pay for the free lunch.

I think this is one of the fundamental problems between teenagers and their parents. The parents are buying the lunch and the kids aren't listening to the pitch! (This is the first place where both parents and teens need to start thinking along the same lines.) So, the point with these two rules: Always know who's doing the selling and know what the price is. *Think about what the transaction is.* What is this person going to do and what are they going to expect me to do?

There is always a price, whether it is money, time, attention, or affection. Look at any situation and try figure out who the seller is and what the transaction is. Get good at doing this because it is very important.

Right now, I am selling you these ideas and the price is the time it takes you to read these pages (along with the cost of the book). My ideas, you reading these pages—that's the transaction. You read and I try to convince you that what I'm saying makes sense and can help you be more successful. Once you've finished reading, the deal is over: I got your attention and you chose to believe me, not believe me, or simply not to care. I don't owe you anymore, and you don't owe me, so *I will leave you alone*. That's how the world works—everything has a price, everything is a transaction. If you pay the price, you get the goodies. If you don't pay someone what you owe them, they won't leave you alone! This is the simple part. The hard part is that people almost always disagree on what is owed and what's been paid.

KNOW WHAT YOU OWE!

Teachers probably bug you about a poor job you did on a test or a paper. The transaction in this case: They teach and you learn. They think that you owe them more than you paid, so they bug you about it. They think they got taken, exactly the same as if they were only paid $50 for a $100 skateboard. People are not nice when they think they've been taken. They are angry! Forget about whether it's fair or not!

Ditch Wish

One day I ditched school with my friends Cody and Graham, and I'm pretty sure Max was there too! At the end of the day, we went back down to school so we could get picked up by our parents. Cody wanted to go really quick to get something out of his locker and asked if anybody wanted to go with him, and I was like, "Sure, I'll go with you." So, I went over there, and he went and got his books, and we were leaving, and I saw my French teacher, which is also his Spanish teacher. She asked us both why we weren't in class, and Cody, being the smart kid he is, said we both had a doctor's appointment! This made it pretty obvious that we had ditched school. She calls into the office and she asks them if we were absent from any of our other classes, and finds out that we didn't go to any of them. So she calls our parents personally and says, "Oh, these kids ditched school!" I got caught, and Max got caught. Because Cody got caught, Cody's mom told Graham's mom, and Graham got caught. So in the end, we all got caught. We wanted something, we wanted to not go to school—to have a good time, but we wanted it for nothing. We didn't want to have to face the consequences. So, we're all bummed at our teacher, but being mad at her is really the wrong thing, because she was just doing her job. I should have realized that there were going to be some consequences, and next time, I'll be sure *not* to run into my French teacher! No, next time, I shouldn't ditch school, because, although I want something for nothing, I should realize that nothing's for nothing, you don't get anything for nothing, you have to think about what's going to happen. I'm grounded for a month, and if somebody told me that one day was going to cost a whole month, I'd be all like, "No way!" but that's how stuff always works out.

Nate—16

Getting people to leave you alone is about paying them off, and the only way to do that *is to pay them what they think you owe them, not what you think!* This is not fair! So what? It's the way the world is.

Think about it. If you go into a store to buy a candy bar, you pay them what *they* decided to charge, not what you think it's worth. You don't argue with them. You don't discuss the candy bar, what it cost to make, and why you only have so much money. You either pay and get the candy, or you don't. You know this rule. It's like being offside in soccer. Why is it so hard to apply this rule to all the transactions that take place in your life? Obligations and relationships work exactly that way. It's really very simple. Know what the price is and be willing to pay, willing to do the work. When was the last time you bought something without knowing the price, without knowing how much it would cost?

So, now you know how to get people to leave you alone. It works every time. There are no free lunches, everyone is selling and buying, and it takes far less effort to pay what someone thinks you owe than to fight about it. Next time just ask someone who's bugging you, "What do you think I owe you?" Then be willing to pay up. Don't argue about the price. It's done. They will leave you alone! If you're dead set to try to convince that person that the candy bar is only worth ten cents, then they won't leave you alone—and ultimately them bugging you is the price *you* have to pay.

It's the same with the price you have to pay to your parents. You resent the fact that you owe your parents more than you will ever be able to pay, and you want out of the transaction ("I didn't *ask* to be born"). It doesn't matter, you're here and you *do* owe. The key thing with your parents is that they are the *only* ones in whole world who really don't expect to be paid back. The only thing they really want as "payment" is your success and appreciation. They want to see that you are at least trying to do the best you can, and that you don't just appear to be "entitled" to all the stuff they have had to work very, very hard for. *They want to see that you're working as hard as they are!* This is the only reward they are looking for, and when you think about it, it really isn't all that much! This too, is a Fact of Life.

❊   ❊   ❊

KEY POINTS
You should now see that the free lunch is never free. It's a joke. There are big rules and medium rules and small rules in life. Knowing what they are and thinking about them will make you

more money, make you happier, and make you have more fun. "Buying and selling" is a good thing. There is always a transaction taking place and it is a valuable skill to get good at identifying your own personal transactions. Seeing the world as a series of transactions helps you to better understand the prices that are always set by the person doing the selling. Paying the price that is charged gets people off your back. Pretty simple stuff, but you probably never thought about it this way. Get used to thinking like this. Not necessarily agreeing with me, but looking at simple stuff with a critical eye.

❊ ❊ ❊

You should now spend a little time talking about this:

- Do you think that there is always a price to be paid, always a transaction going on?
- What do you think about the rules? Can you come up with some big, medium, and small rules?
- Do you think that someone is always selling and someone is always buying?
- Do you think that it's easier to simply pay what you owe than to fight about it?
- Can you see how knowing the price up front makes everything more fair?
- Do you think that this can help you understand the world and get more out of it?
- Do you think there is more in this book that can be helpful?

life's a bitch, then you die!

(How to See The Big Picture)

The previous section was about rules and transactions. It was about how you should be thinking about *your* place in life—what's expected of you. This section is devoted to what you can expect from life and how you should think about these expectations—The Big Picture. In addition, you get to use some of the nifty visual aids!

SPEAK THE TRUTH, BUT LEAVE IMMEDIATELY AFTER!

Before we leap into this point, we need to think a bit about "generalizations" and "specifics," and how they should fit into the thinking process. As previously discussed, we've seen that we are taught certain lessons early on in life that hurt our ability to think well. Such is the case with generalizations. The *Microsoft Encarta College Dictionary* defines "generalization" as "a statement or conclusion that is derived from and applies equally to a number of cases." In other words, something can be generally true, but not always. I will use specifics to refer to specific instances that are not general in nature.

For example, you can generalize that men are stronger than women. This is a true generalization, but any specific woman may be stronger than any specific man. This means that you can have two true statements that contradict each other. Men are generally stronger than women, but Martha is stronger than Sam. We are taught that generalizations about people are bad ("Don't label me! That's prejudice! You sexist pig!"). Once again, these statements tend to make us bad thinkers because seeing generalizations and patterns in life is immensely important and helpful. The harm always comes from applying a generalization to a specific case. Because men are generally stronger than women, Martha *can't* be stronger than Sam. Bad thinking! Sam can get the crap kicked out of him with this type of thinking. Although men are generally stronger than women, Martha can still be stronger than Sam. Good thinking. Know the generalization *and* the specific.

Most generalizations are about groups of people: Jocks are dumb, cheerleaders are oversexed, and nerds immature. These may or may not be *generally* true, but even if they are, some jocks are smart, some cheerleaders are virgins, and some nerds quite sophisticated. Keep in mind that *you* are "known" by the generalizations people have about the group you choose to associate with, even though it may not apply specifically to you. This is a big part of seeing The Big Picture, and is discussed in more detail in section seven.

Just as you can generalize about groups, you can also generalize about certain things that you should expect about life, things that will probably happen to you! You will probably graduate from high school. You will probably get married. Keep in mind that while these things generally happen, you will not always be able to count on them in the specific case of your individual day-to-day life. Regardless, if you see what's likely to be coming at you, you can be better prepared to deal with it. This is what tornado warnings are for.

TAKING YOUR BEST SHOT!

Basketball can show you how to be prepared for something that's likely to happen. You may be good at a particular shot, say from the baseline or top of the key. These are referred to as your "percentage" shots. You have better odds at making these shots than you do at making others, and you may even have the best odds of making these shots as anyone else on your team. This means that when your team is down by one point, with only five seconds to go in the game, the coach may set up a play for you to be in your percentage shot position. Does it mean that you will make the shot? No, it simply means that you, your coach, and your team are going with the percentages; taking literally their "best shot." They are seeing what's coming up (the tornado warning) and taking their best collective shot (getting ready for it). This concept (kind of a "generalization of a generalization") is critical in life, as every day you are faced with little situations where you need to take your best shot. Knowing what's coming up and what to do about it will make you more successful. This is all about thinking ahead and being prepared.

Knowing the odds of certain things happening can help you get in the best position to score your percentage shots. If you go with the odds, you will score more points in life, and this translates to more wins, more money, more fun, and more satisfaction. Simple stuff. In business, there is a concept called "reaction time." If you have a plan for accomplishing a certain task (getting prepared for something coming up), you build reaction time into this plan. This way, when things start to go wrong, as they do with every plan, you know *early* enough so that you have time to make the necessary changes—time to react to the problem and fix it. This works really well with life too!

Mañana

God, you really shouldn't put things off dude. I mean, like you think there's so much time for stuff, but it's like, I don't know, things just happen, then all of the sudden the time is just totally gone. Like I'm 18 now, and I still don't have a driver's license. I could have got one when I was 16, but you had to do that school and everything, and my folks were not really into giving me all the money I needed for it, so I thought I'd just chill and wait, because when you're 18, you don't need the school and stuff. So now my folks are just totally pissed whenever I need to get somewhere, and they like want me to get a job and stuff, but then I can't get to the places I need to go to get the applications. So I waited, and my friends will like give me a ride to someplace they're going, but if I want to go down to turn in an application, they're all like, "No way, dude!" I don't even have the money to pay for their gas and stuff, so I'm just like waiting around, and I don't have a job, and I don't have any money, and I don't have a car, and I don't have a license, and everybody's all, "So, what're you gonna do?" And I'm all like, "I don't know dude, I thought I had all this time and everything."

Robert—18

TIME IS *NOT* ON YOUR SIDE!

Keeping this in mind, let's get out the yardstick you hopefully have at hand. (In the introduction to this book, I mentioned several items you need to have ready when reading this book. If you don't, please take a look at the list and round up this stuff before you go on.)

OK, so *now* you have the yardstick. Lay it down on a table so that everyone can see it. We are going to use the yardstick as a timeline for you and your parent's life. We are going to imagine that each inch on the yardstick is equal to ten years. The entire yardstick equals three hundred sixty years. Yeesh, a very long time. If you imagine that the thirty-six–inch mark is today, the other end of the yardstick represents the year 1643, roughly twenty years after the Pilgrims landed at Plymouth Rock. World War II started only six inches ago. I mention this to give you some perspective. We have all done timelines for school at some point or another, but I doubt that you have really ever thought about your own personal timeline or how it fits in with your family.

Light bulbs should be flashing all over the place right now! You know, those cartoon light bulbs that go off when the character has an idea. You should be looking at the yardstick and thinking that your entire life is generally only about seven or eight inches long (seventy to eighty years)! Not much! Some people may make it to ten inches (one hundred years), but not many. Some people die or get killed early on, at only one or two inches. You should start learning how to think about what you can do to get the most out of your seven or eight inches—because the clock is ticking. You've already used up almost two inches, and you only have about five or six more to go. Your parents have used up four or five inches and only have about three inches left! Wow!

This should be insightful to you because at your age (pretty much any age before you hit forty), most people don't think too much about time as it relates to their life. In fact, they think that they are pretty much immortal, that they will never really die. Death is not a pleasant thought, and our society really doesn't deal very well with it, but this is one of the *certain* expectations you can have about life. You're only around for a while, and as is best said in an ancient Jewish proverb, "You are dead a *very* long time." In other words, in comparison to how long you are going to be dead, life is pretty short.

This kind of awareness can become a big motivator in how you spend your time. If you are lucky, you will get the maximum seven or eight inches—and remember, there are no "do-overs." Even more important, there is no guarantee that you'll get all of your anticipated seven or eight inches. Stepping into a car with a drunk driver may take care of whatever portion you have left. I have digressed here because its important to think about life as something very precious, all the more so because it has an expiration date. No need to be depressed about it, or act like a "deer in headlights," or ignore it—just know it for what it is, the great motivator!

Now we should examine what generally goes on for everyone's seven or eight inches. For the most part, you can expect the following from each of your inches—each of your ten year decades. This is not intended to be exact or specific; these are just certain generalizations or expectations you can have about each decade to make you better prepared.

Period	Age	Theme	Expectation
First Decade	(0–9)	Sponge Brain	Here you are just absorbing the world and trying to figure out how you fit in.
Second Decade	(10–19)	Look at Me!	Here you've mastered how you think you fit in, and are now trying to show everyone how much you know. Look what I can do, coming of age!
Third Decade	(20–29)	On Your Own	Here you go out in the world on your own. Odds are you will get married and have children in this inch.
Fourth Decade	(30–39)	Family Hell	Here, you have your own kids and learn about all the responsibility your parents are always talking about. It is exhausting!
Fifth Decade	(40–49)	See Ya!	After surviving Family Hell, it's mid-life crisis time, and here is when you might want to be on your own again. These are divorce-prone years.

Period	Age	Theme	Expectation
Sixth Decade	(50–59)	Granny Bound	Your kids start their own families, and you get to finally know everything there is to know, or so you think!
Seventh Decade	(60+)	Waiting to Die	Basically, here you are just putting in time, trying to do all the stuff you missed out on in the previous six inches.

This is all a little tongue in cheek, but it focuses on what you should be thinking about, how you should think about it, and how the pieces are connected. This is generally the stuff you can expect to happen to you. This is The Big Picture. Knowing what is probably coming up will make you better prepared to face the future and succeed. You can pretty much plan on this stuff, but there is a little counterintuitive twist that I want to point out. Knowing what's coming up is one thing, but doing the right things *at the right time* has huge benefits.

SIZE *DOES* MATTER

We probably all remember being a kid at an amusement park and getting measured to see if we could go on the roller coaster, standing there, embarrassed, stretching ourselves to the limit. The height restriction obviously exists for safety and insurance reasons, but it's also about what we're mentally and emotionally ready for. If you go on a "big kid" roller coaster when you're too young, it can scare the crap out of you and take the fun out of all your future roller coaster rides. Without really doing too much thinking about it, and with a valid safety concern, the world has decided that you shouldn't do certain things until you are big enough to do them. This makes us really mad because we always think we are bigger than we really are. This is a good Life Lesson to remember. You are *never* as big as you think you are!

A couple of things result from this issue of time; how long you have been on this planet, your age, and how big you are. First, to prove how big you think you are, you are always trying to cheat the system—stand on your toes to get on the ride, sneak into an R-rated movie, drive your dad's car, or get drunk. You are always trying to do things the world has decided you are not big enough to do and you're trying to show them how wrong they are. Second, you should discover that when you try to do something you're not really big enough for, you are usually really bad at it and you get in a lot of trouble. Some trouble comes from just being stupid, but if you think about it, most trouble comes from trying to do things you are not ready for ("Whoa, I didn't expect that!").

A good example is having children. If you wait until your mid to late twenties to have your own kids, you have the best odds of being as good a parent as you can be (a good percentage shot). You have the right combination of energy (you're still pretty young), money (you're just now starting to earn a decent wage), and experience (you're finally ready for this level of responsibility). If you have a child when you're still a teenager, you don't have the right combination going for you. You have way too much energy, no dough, a whole basket full of "wrong" expectations, and not enough experience. The counterintuitive thought here is that you not only screw up this period of your life, but also the period in the future when you *should* be doing those things. By having to take care of an infant as a teen, you would not only miss out on those really fun early twenties where you will be on your own for the first time, but you would also screw up your early thirties. When you reach your early thirties, you will finally start to have some freedom because your kid will no longer be so demanding, and just as you are ready to make up for some lost party time, you'll find that all your friends are now starting their own families and are not interested in the party scene anymore—been there, done that!

Too Cool for School

I remember this kid, he was a freshman. He's like this little, skinny guy, looked pretty lame. So he tries out for the tennis team. Anyway, he comes out and doesn't know anybody, and starts to play, and nobody's really paying any attention, and he's great. He's got the really big serve, and he gets to everything.

So, we're all warming up and hitting the ball. Coach Tanner yells over at Karl, one of the best players on varsity, to come hit with the kid. So Karl starts hitting with him, and the kid is kicking his ass, passing shots, killer lobs and everything. So, the season starts and Coach Tanner ends up putting him on the Varsity team in the number two singles spot. The kid does great, and wins a bunch of matches. I was kind of pissed, because I was a sophomore and played JV, but this kid was really good.

Anyway, the season's over and everybody goes back to life. The next year, we all come out for the team again, and there's like all these new kids—some freshmen, and some who have transferred from other schools. There's this big new development where we live, and I guess a bunch of kids moved in.

Anyway, the kid is still really good, but there's all these other kids that are really good too. It's like such a bust, because I'm thinking that I'm going to have to play JV again, and I really wanted to be on varsity. So we all go through tryouts and everybody's really strong, and it ends up that a bunch of kids that played last year get cut, and a bunch of the new kids end up on varsity. The little skinny kid from the year before makes the team, but doesn't make varsity, he gets put on JV. I got cut and was really bummed.

Anyway, I find out that the skinny kid goes nuts because he's not on varsity, and ends up quitting the team. I found this out because Coach Tanner called me, and I got his spot. I thought it was so cool because I really wanted to play, and even though

I wasn't on varsity, I was still on the team, and I had one more year and everything.

Anyway, I thought about the kid that quit, and I felt really bad for him. He was really good, and probably would have made varsity his junior year, but I guess he was just too into himself or something. I mean, if he had played JV as a freshman, he probably would have been happy to play JV again as a sophomore, but because he played varsity, I guess he thought it was lame.

Anyway, he quit, and I see him around school hanging out with this loser group of kids, and I think that this really changed his life. I mean, he was really good, and being on the team and everything would have been cool, but he thought it was some big bust, and probably didn't play tennis anymore. That was messed up.

Connor – 17

HOW TIME FLIES

Looking at your whole life and planning to do things at the right time and in the right order is a really good strategy. Getting things all mixed up and out of order screws up the time you're in as well as the time you should be doing something else. This works on a big scale and on a little scale. When you're 17, be content to do a good job at being 17, don't try to be 20! You'll do a horrible job of it, and when you are 20, then what?

Now back to the yardstick. If you think about it, the reason your parents won't let you do certain things is because they are trying to keep you in order, trying to keep you doing the right things at the right time. You get mad about this because you think you are so big and that they just don't understand. This conflict invariably results in your enraged admonishment, "Yeah, well you did that when you were my age, and you turned out OK!"

Let's be a little counterintuitive about this thought process. Remember, things are never as you first think they are. Kids are always using the "you turned out OK" premise, as well as the "everybody else is doing it" premise. Ask yourself what this really has to do with you. Because Albert Einstein failed math in elementary school, will you be an Einstein too? No! Your seven or eight inches are yours and yours alone, and have absolutely nothing to do with anyone else's seven or eight inches. Regardless of what anyone else has done, or is allowed to do, your restrictions (things you are not allowed to do) are put forward by your parents to make sure you are taking your percentage shots—doing the right things at the right times for you!

You need to relax and not be in such a hurry to do things before you're ready, no matter how ready you think you are. You should be spending this energy on getting prepared for what's coming at you instead of trying to do so much! It's like washing a car. If you spend a few minutes planning, getting all the stuff you'll need together before you start, the job is much quicker and easier. Why don't we do this with life? Spend a little more time thinking and planning, and you'll find you're not running around so aimlessly. Your parents are really trying to help you with this. They have a better perspective on life because they've been around for three or four more inches than you have. They also have to remember what it was like as a teenager. Time goes much faster for parents than it does for teenagers, and this is another good thing to keep in mind.

HOW TIME WORKS

Although we all know that a year has 365 days (except leap year), and a day has 24 hours, with 60 minutes in each hour, and 60 seconds in each minute, we don't really "feel" time this way. We feel time as a *percentage* of how long we've been around on this planet. When you are three years old, a year is one third of your whole life. When you're thirty, one year is only a thirtieth of your life. A thirtieth is a lot smaller than a third, so time seems to speed up. Each year becomes a smaller and smaller percentage of your whole life. When you're fifteen, a year is a fifteenth of your life, but you're smart enough to know that you've got about sixty years left. The problem is that you think each of these sixty years is going to be like the one you just had, the fifteenth! You think you've got sixty fifteenths left. This thinking makes you think your life will be four times longer than it really will be. Time speeds up. This is a good thing to be thinking about.

When your parents say "maybe next year," you cringe that that is so far away. It's much shorter to them. You need to think about "parent years" and they need to think about "teenage years" (kind of like dog years). Realize that time will speed up for you, and that "next year" comes faster and faster!

* * *

Key Points

Seeing The Big Picture in life, really getting a handle on how you are going to go about your seven or eight inches here, is about several things. It's about generalizations and knowing when they apply and when they don't. It's about knowing what your percentage shots are and when the best time is to take them. It's about anticipating what's coming up. When you think about The Big Picture, you should think about your timeline and your own "expiration date." You should be thinking about what you should be doing in each of your decades and being patient enough to *do things in order*. You should understand that you will never be as "big" as you think you are! Once you are able to see your life this way, it will be much easier to figure out what you should be doing. What you should be doing is getting ready for what you can anticipate is coming up in your life. Seeing The Big Picture is truly the first step in being "big" yourself!

* * *

You should now spend a little time talking about this:

- What do you think about generalizations? Can you come up with some?
- What are your percentage shots, the things you are good at?

- How do you feel about your seven or eight inches and about your "expiration date"?
- Do you see why it's a good idea to be doing the right things at the right time?
- Do you see how silly it is to always be trying to be so big?
- Do you see how time changes as you get older, how it speeds up?

it's not the size of the ship, but the motion of the ocean!

(How to Get the Most Out of What You've Got)

This Fact of Life about the size of the ship is an old joke about sex. Women typically use this line when joking about the size of a man's "equipment," so to speak. The Fact of Life within this joke is its deeper meaning. What it's really saying is, "It's not what you have, but how you use it." In this context, it is a very important guideline for life. I use the joking form only to help you remember it.

YOU CAN'T TEACH A PIG TO SING: IT FRUSTRATES YOU, AND ANNOYS THE PIG!

One of the great Life Lessons is that you will always get further ahead using poor tools well than you will using great tools poorly. In other words, a fine craftsman who has a poor set of tools may have the ability to produce beautiful work with a little skill and creativity. Imagine the ancient wonders of the world that were produced with little more than stone implements (take the time to visit an exhibition of ancient Egyptian, Greek, or Roman art). Likewise, you can put the finest set of tools modern man can produce into the hands of an idiot and he or she will invariably produce something ridiculous. A fine set of tools in the hands of a superb craftsman can replace a heart valve. With this clearly in your mind, you can see the importance of becoming a craftsman. I'm not talking about how you use physical tools, but how you use your brain. Indeed, you can become very skilled at the way you use your ability to think. With a little practice and effort, you will be much better off than someone who may have more raw intelligence than you, but not the *discipline* to use that intelligence effectively. This is all about getting the most out of what you've got. You can make a little go a long way if you're clever about it, and being clever is not all that hard to do.

R-E-S-P-E-C-T

I remember getting ready to graduate from high school. I was thinking about my life, and where I was going to go, and what was going to happen to me, and I realized that I really didn't have a very good handle on how things worked. I was thinking about what life was all about, and it hit me, one of those moments when you think of something pretty simple, but it has a really big impact on the way you live. What I realized is that the one thing, really the only thing that *everybody* is interested in is respect. That's what it's all about. If you look at anyone, anywhere, the only thing they're all really trying to do is get a little respect. The way they act, the way they do things, the jobs they have, who they go out with, everything—it all has to do with respect, getting the respect from the people you want it from.

This was a big moment for me, kind of like opening my eyes for the first time. I know that there's a bunch of things that motivate people, like love and hate and sex and greed, but you can always boil everything down to respect—what you get, and what you give. I had this all rolling around in my head, and then another thought came to me, and this thought was even bigger! Not only is it all about respect, but the point is that as you grow older and become more mature, you realize that the things that people respect changes. As people get older, their values change, and when their values change, it changes the things they respect. What kids respect in high school is how cool or popular someone is, how they look, or who they hang with, or their car, or something. When you get out of high school, you find out that nobody really cares how cool you are anymore. People who are older, who have finished high school, respect what someone does, what kind of job they have, how successful you've been at doing whatever it is you do. It's like you're playing some kind of game, and suddenly, all the rules are changed. Like ditching school was so cool and reckless and made you a big shot in high school, but now, ditching work just gets you fired.

In high school, being all cool and detached and not caring about anything made you so popular, but in the real world, if you're all detached and don't care, nobody really notices anymore, because everyone's so busy doing real stuff . Realizing that this was what was going on was a big moment in my life, a moment I know I'll always remember. It was like suddenly, something clicked and I understood. It was kind of like one of those algebra problems that you just don't get and then you do, and you can't figure out how you were not able to get it in the first place.

Kevin—19

So, the best way to go about getting clever, getting the most out of what you've got, is to get good at seeing the things that need to be done, and then figuring out how to do them. I saw a TV show on how the great Pyramids in Egypt were supposedly built. They took a modern, skilled stone mason from Ohio, a structural engineer from a prestigious school, an Egyptologist, and several other experts to Egypt. On a small plot of ground, they were asked to build a thirty-foot tall pyramid using only the tools the ancient Egyptians had. After several weeks and many entertaining arguments, the experts were unable to accomplish this relatively simple task (in comparison to the soaring structures built three thousand years ago). The ancient Egyptians were very, very good at seeing what needed to be done and had the ability to figure out how to go about it—getting, by far, the most out of what they had!

NO MATTER WHERE YOU GO, THERE YOU ARE!

Let's start here by going back to the yardstick to figure out what it is that you have to work with. To begin, you first need to figure out both who and where you are. Take out the yardstick (with the hole in one end), the foam poster board, the thumb tack, and the pencil. In roughly the center of the poster board, tack the yardstick down by placing the tack through the hole in its end. The yardstick should now be able to rotate around the board, much like the hour hand of a clock. With the yardstick pointing in any direction, find the five-inch mark (a number just picked at random), and place the tip of the pencil at this measurement on the poster board. We'll pretend that this five-inch mark is the year your father was born. If he is in his mid 40s he has traveled four and a half inches of his life (remember that each inch represents ten years). This four and a half inches is not a straight line because everyone changes their direction in life quite a bit. So, move the yardstick slowly up and down the poster board while you let the pencil trace out the line from the five-inch mark to the nine and a half inch mark (see figure 1).

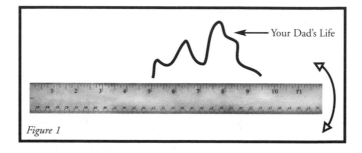

Figure 1

Move the yardstick out of the way and look at the squiggly line that you've drawn. This squiggly line represents your father's life so far. Now you can move the yardstick back to where it was and find the point at eight inches where the yardstick intersects the squiggly line. If your father was about thirty years old when you were born, this becomes the point where your own squiggly line began. You can now trace out your life by letting the yardstick move around while you move the pencil from the eight inch mark to the nine and a half inch mark. This is your life (see figure 2). If you are so inclined, you can make squiggles for any brothers or sisters as well as your mother. These lines represent the members of your family as they have moved through life so far.

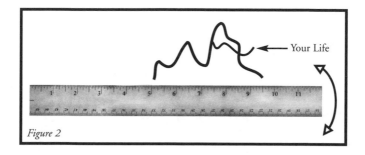

Figure 2

What does this all mean? It means a couple of things. For starters, like finger prints, no two squiggles are ever the same. They never start at the same place at the same time or move in the same directions. Every squiggle for every person who ever lived could be represented on a large enough poster board. If you figure that modern humans have been on this planet in their current form for about thirty thousand years, you could use a ruler three thousand inches long (about the length of a football field) to make squiggles for everyone. Now imagine a poster board and a ruler the size of a football field, and then imagine what your roughly inch-and-a-half squiggle would look like on that football-field-sized poster board. Picturing this, you could see exactly where you are in the jumble of every human being who has ever lived. Your inch and a half doesn't take up too much space out there. Remember, no one was ever born in exactly the same place at exactly the same time. Even twins, from the moment they are born, start moving in slightly different directions, making slightly different squiggles.

There are two Life Lessons that you can take away from this picture of humanity. First, any little seven- or eight-inch squiggle on that football field is pretty damn small. No one should take themselves all that seriously! Second, and perhaps more important, this view should dispel forever the teenage desire to compare their squiggle to any other one on the field. What I'm saying relates to the comments all teenagers have all made, "Well when you were my age, you…" or "But Jimmy did a lot worse than I did." Forget about it—that is bad thinking and bad logic. No squiggles are ever the same, and no comparisons between squiggles make any sense at all! So what! Everyone starts in a different place on the field and moves in different directions as different things happen to them. If you want to compare yourself to Jimmy, why not Jesus or Napoleon? It makes the same amount of sense. You are a lone, little squiggle on a very big football field. You may not like this view of things, but it is reality. The sooner you accept this Fact of Life, the better chance you are going to have of making your squiggle as significant and fulfilling as it can be for *you*. It's about how you can get the most out of what you've got, and you start by seeing how unique you are.

CONNECT THE DOTS

There is another Life Lesson to be drawn from this exercise, which you should incorporate into your World View. This lesson is not very popular because it involves an obligation, and no one likes obligations. If you imagine this great football field of squiggles, you would be able to walk out there and trace your squiggle all the way back to the very first squiggle. Like with your father's squiggle and yours, you started at a point in his life when you were born. Likewise, his squiggle started at a point in his father's life when he was born, and so on. Every squiggle of each of the six *billion* people alive today could be traced back to the very first human with an unbroken line. Every squiggle that you are connected to forms an unbroken line of survival from the very beginning. If anyone died before having children, their genes were eliminated from the football field forever, folks who were just a little too slow to outwit the saber-toothed tiger, or the dummies who failed to put enough food away for the winter.

Imagine all the trouble these people went through so that you could be alive today. You should feel some kind of an obligation to keep the line moving, and to keep it moving well. It's like a relay race. Thirty thousand years of people went though God knows what to place the baton of your genes in your hands, and you are the current pay off for all this effort. What you do, where you end up, and how you are able to create yet another squiggle on the field are the result of all those years of effort. If you want, you can take this even further and imagine that the squiggles go all the way back to the very first living thing on this planet. Six billion years of pretty horrifying trouble and survival have resulted in your birth. Your obligation is somewhat bigger than just yourself or your parents.

DON'T THINK THERE ARE NO CROCODILES BECAUSE THE WATER IS CALM

To keep the analogy alive, let's imagine this football field as a great sea instead of a poster board. You start out in a little boat dropped in the water from your parent's bigger boat. Imagine your boat as about half an inch long out in this football field. We start out as a little boat on this vast ocean, and each of our boats are as different as the time and place they were first dunked in the water. Some people are lucky and start out with totally cool little boats that we can imagine are faster, more safe, and sleek (the lucky ones who are smarter, stronger, or better off), and of course, some people start out in pretty crappy little boats (the unlucky ones who aren't quite as sharp, a little bit weaker, or poor).

You can imagine the condition of your boat as the condition in which your life began. When you look at it this way, there's even less of a reason to try to compare yourself or your situation in life to anyone else—you started at different places, different times, going different directions, and were given different tools to work with. The initial condition of your boat is unique.

This again is part of the general "unfairness" of life. For every boat on the football-field-sized ocean, there are better boats and there are worse boats. Imagine the condition of someone's boat who was born impoverished and crippled in rural China—not a very good boat. Imagine the boats that Bill Gates's children get. There are a lot of different boats out there on this football field—six billion of them! The point here is to stop complaining about the condition of your boat or where it's at on the football field. There is absolutely nothing you can ever do to change where you started and what you had to work with. Some folks get a lot more, and some folks get a lot less. So what!

What you *can* do however, is determine where your boat is going and what steps you can take to improve it. In fact, every effort you make in life should be with this in mind! *Everything you do either improves or harms your boat.* This is also a Fact of Life. Not only is your boat all you've got, but you're only going to have it for about seven or eight inches. Take very good care of it.

The trick to getting the most out of what you have is to see clearly what needs to be done. Just like a pilot who does a visual inspection of his airplane before entering the cockpit, you should make a visual inspection of your boat. Look at yourself really hard and see what needs attention. I doubt anyone would honestly claim to be perfect, so something could use some effort—and here comes the really cool part. To figure out what you need to do, *you have to have a destination.* Lo and behold, just like the pilot of the airplane, or the captain of the ship, there's really no point to inspecting or repairing anything unless you are going somewhere.

Here you get to be the master of your destiny, and this is the first decision in your life that you are going to make totally on your own. No matter what anyone may think, no one can force your hand in the direction that you end up taking. Oh yeah, your parents, or maybe a few teachers will say that you should do this or you should do that, but no matter how much they yack, they cannot force you, and they certainly are not going to the same place themselves.

It's your boat, your squiggle, and it's totally up to you to figure out where you're going. This seems like a huge thing and it can be intimidating. Oh my God, what great big "purpose" am I supposed to have—to be the president, an astronaut, a professional soccer player? This is where most people get hung up. Obviously, we all feel that we are of immeasurable importance. We're probably the most important thing in the world to ourselves, ("What does this mean for *me*?") so we think we should have some really important goal or purpose. Too much! Overload. As Chairman Mao said, "The longest journey begins with just one step." The trick is to take that step in the general direction you hope to go.

Think of life as a series of connecting flights on an airplane, steps in getting to your final destination. If, for example, you generally want to have the freedom of having extra cash laying around, you will need to have some kind of job that makes good money. If you want a job that makes good money, you will have a better chance if you get the best education you can. To get the best education you can, you need to get the best grades you can. In order to get the best grades you can, you will need to work hard on next week's assignments. To get the best grades on those assignments, you should do the book report early so that you can study more for the tests on Friday. You can take a big, general goal and break it down into smaller and smaller bites until you have a course of action for tomorrow. What direction are you going to go tomorrow? Is that closer to your chosen goal, or further away? *This is the key to getting the most out of what you've got, and how best to improve your boat.*

IF WE DON'T CHANGE DIRECTION SOON, WE'LL END UP WHERE WE'RE GOING

Imagine you are alone in a tiny boat in the middle of the South Pacific (might as well pick a nice ocean). Do you think you would be paying attention to what you were doing there? Do you think you would take stock of what you had on hand, the condition of the boat, and most importantly, where the hell you were going? I would hope so!

Now imagine yourself in this position when all of the sudden a much bigger, older ship pulls up next to you with an experienced captain on board, someone who's been at sea for forty or fifty years. The captain yells down at you, "Hey, you should be going that way, there's land over there, and I would take a look at your rudder, because it looks like some bolts are loose."

Would you be thinking that this guy is a jerk? My guess is that you would probably be pretty damn happy for the company and you would immediately take a look at the bolts on your rudder. You would probably ask how far away that land was and whether there were any tricks to finding it. It's not a matter of pride or ego—it's just common sense, especially if you were all alone out in the ocean. When you are in a dangerous situation, you should be glad for all the help you can get. Let me tell you, being alone out in the real world is a very dangerous situation. There's a lot that can happen in this mean, nasty old world. It makes the South Pacific look like a piece of cake.

All Ashore

My Dad took me, my brother, and my sister to Catalina on his boat. Catalina is an island off Southern California. This is a while ago, but we got there and got a mooring. They don't have docks there. You have to tie up to a buoy sort of thing and take your dinghy if you want to go to shore. They also have water taxis. Anyway, we were hanging around, swimming, doing a little fishing, and my Dad tells us to get ready, that we're going ashore to have dinner at this Italian restaurant, so we get ready and take the dinghy. It was really nice out and the restaurant is a really good one.

So, we're having dinner and talking about stuff, and there's these people at this other table, and they're looking at us, and this woman comes over and gives my Dad this bottle of wine. She said that we all looked so nice together or something. Anyway, my Dad thanks her, and we go back to dinner. When we were done eating, my Dad had finished the bottle of wine, and I guess he was a little drunk, so we leave the restaurant and kind of walk around a little, and it's probably about 10:00 or so.

My Dad tells us to get in the dinghy and go back to the boat, that he's going to have a drink, and he'll take the water taxi back around midnight. He tells us about channel nine on the radio, and how we can get in touch with the Harbor Patrol, and that we should just put in a tape and watch a movie until he gets back, and to just stay on the boat.

So, we all go back and settle in to watch a movie, and my sister starts to not feel very good. She says she's going to throw up, and we get her to the side of the boat, and she hurls.

My brother and I are wondering what to do, and we get this lame idea that we should get in the dinghy and go find my Dad. It's pretty dark around the boat, and we get the dinghy going, and tell my sister to take it easy, that we'll be right back. We're going for a few minutes, when all of the sudden there's this big light on us, and this guy on a bull horn asking us what we're doing. He's a Harbor Patrol guy, and we tell him about my Dad and my sister, and that we're going to get him. He asked us what my Dad had told us to do. We say that he told us to wait on the boat. He asks us why we're not waiting on the boat, and we just kind of look at each other. He told us to go back, and told us to call him on channel nine if my sister wasn't feeling better, so we went back.

My sister was fine by now, but my brother and me were still figuring that we needed to do something, so we got my Dad's cell phone, and called my Mom back at home. My Mom doesn't like boats very much, and she sort of freaked when we told her that we were alone. Anyway, it wasn't very long after this that my Dad came back. We didn't tell him anything, but just as he was getting off the taxi, the Harbor Patrol boat came up, and the guy told my Dad what happened, and was kind of laughing. My Dad asked about my sister, and he told the Harbor Patrol guy everything was fine and thanks. He asked us why we just didn't do what he told us, and we said we didn't know, but we didn't tell him about calling our Mom.

A little bit later the cell phone rings and it's our Mom and she's screaming at my Dad—we can hear her over the phone. My Mom and Dad had just got divorced, and they weren't getting along very well. When he gets off the phone, he tells us that it would have been nice to tell him that we'd called her.

Anyway, when we got back from Catalina, there was this big deal with the divorce lawyers and everything, and it was a big bust for my Dad. Looking back, it really wasn't a big deal that he sent us to the boat alone, I mean, we were old enough, and had been there a bunch of times. If we'd just done what my Dad had said, or if we had just done what the Harbor Patrol guy had said, it wouldn't have been a big deal, but we got all wrapped up in needing to do something, and kind of really messed things up. It was pretty stupid, and ended up being a big problem for my Dad. Anyway, sometimes people tell you stuff, and you think you know better. You usually don't!

Ben–17

People giving you advice on where you might want to go or things you could be doing should be viewed as a welcome gift, a great way to get the most out of what you've got. After all, it's totally up to you what advice you take and what advice you ignore. The smart move is to listen carefully to any advice ever offered and ask questions. If you don't understand something, get to the bottom of it. Why should I be doing what you are suggesting? Imagine the questions you would have for the captain of that bigger boat. How long does it take to get where I'm going, and what's the best way to get there? Is there a better place to go? Is there an easier place to go? What's just over the horizon? Start looking at your life in this manner and all of a sudden the lights will be turned on. You can finally see where you're going!

It should become pretty obvious when you start thinking this way that just like in a foot race, or any race for that matter, it is really not very important where you were or what you had at the start of the race—it's how you finish that matters. No one really cares who was winning for the first couple of laps. It's all about how you end up. In fact, the worse off you were to start with, the bigger the win. Don't you love those stories of the coming-from-behind victories, the injured runner who toughs it out and still wins the race? Rooting for the underdog is ingrained in our culture and for good reason. There are a lot of us, in fact most of us, starting out in these little boats who are total underdogs. We want to root for the folks we can identify with.

It's interesting that the flip side is one of those counterintuitive lessons in life. If we root for the underdog, we despise the overdog, the one with special advantages and excess help. These are the guys the hero has to eventually fight in all the action movies, and although the hero usually gets the crap beat out of him for a few feet of film, he overcomes the odds and prevails against the over-dog. In real life it's the same way. We are pissed off about the poor little rich kids. It makes us mad when people get extra stuff and privileges that we don't. But I think we learn the wrong lesson here.

The counterintuitive way to think about this is that those with special advantages have problems too. There are two things always working against them. First, they have a whole lot of pressure to succeed. After all, they have such a good start, everyone is expecting something great. ("Boy, if I only had that going for me, I'd…") The other thing that works against them is that no victory will ever be sweet enough. No matter what they accomplish, everyone's attitude will be, "So what? Of course they made it, they had all those advantages!"

I mention this counterintuitive side of being an underdog to show you that there's an upside to any disadvantages or extra difficulties you may face. Ending up with a sleek, giant yacht moored in a beautiful, topical harbor will be all the more sweet for having started off as such a tiny, unprepared little skiff. This boat analogy may be getting a bit much by now, but it is a good way to look at things. Of course, I am not really talking about boats nor the material world ("The guy with the most toys wins"). It's not really about the stuff you can touch.

CHARACTER: WHAT YOU DO WHEN YOU THINK NO ONE IS LOOKING

It *is* about the intangible stuff—that is, character. Who would you really like to hang out with more; the rich jerk captain of a big fancy boat he inherited and can't operate, or the salty old mariner with a heart of gold? The condition of the boat is what keeps you alive, but the respect you receive in life is from your seamanship, the way you live your life, your character. People notice someone with character (honor, integrity, compassion) and they respect it. Regardless of how much money or stuff you end up with, this is where real respect comes from. This is something to keep in mind while figuring out where you're going and what repairs or modifications you need to pay attention to—how to get the most out of what you've got.

There's a great sailboat race in New England every year called the Cake-Bread Race. Only the best of the best America's Cup Class captains are invited. Picture those huge, beautiful racing boats smashing through the waves with a crew of six. What's cool about the Cake-Bread Race is that the captains all race alone in little dinghies to prove their seamanship. It's not the size of the ship—it's the motion of the ocean. It's what you do with what you've got!

The point that I really want to drive home is that most kids are always so bummed about how tough stuff is for them, evidently wanting everything to be easier, to waltz through life without any work or effort. We typically learn too late in life that the work and the effort is the fun part. Think about the best stories you hear when people talk about things that happened to them. These stories are mostly about the struggle or work that went on, almost never about how easy something was. ("Let me tell you, that trip to Minneapolis was something else.") *Plan to have some good stories to tell*, and be willing to do the work! Figuring out where you want to go, what direction you need to be pointed in, and what needs to be done in order to get there in one piece is what it's all about. When you've gone through most of your seven or eight inches, you will look back and really understand that *it's not the getting there, but the going that's fun.* HUGE Life Lesson here! The sooner you get this picture, many, many things will fall into place for you.

The more that you can imagine a destination, how and where you want to be living in five, ten, or twenty years, you will find that it's not too hard to get there if you pay attention to your seamanship (navigation) and the condition of your boat. Just imagine the movie you would want to be in. What would you look like? How would you act? Where would you be living? You are going to have to do many things to get there. Be really honest with yourself. Fooling yourself into thinking that everything's just fine will only get you nowhere in a hurry. Also, never forget to have a plan B. Things have a way of not working out the way we plan them, and many times in life you are going to be damn glad you have an escape route.

* * *

Key Points

Conclusion time: How do you get the most out of what you've got? First and foremost, you don't take yourself too seriously. After all, you are only a little squiggle in a vast ocean. Although the initial condition of your boat may not be the greatest, you learn to use the tools you were given and use them the best you can. It is what it is. You think about your connection to all the other squiggles out there and you take a deep breath. You are going to make this work, and you are going to give it your best shot. You're the pay off. A lot of other squiggles went to a lot of trouble to give you this chance.

You are going to have to take a really hard, honest look at the condition of your boat and think about what things you can do to improve it. Remember, every thing you do either helps or hurts the condition of your boat. You are going have to think about where it is you want to end up and what direction you need to be going to get there. You are not going to get overwhelmed by how big your goal or expectations may be. You will just think about that goal generally and break it down into bite-sized chunks, a week or a day at a time.

Once you start, you are going to have to pay attention to your seamanship and think about how you are "spending" your life. You are going to have to pay attention to the way you live each and every day, either getting closer or farther away from what you really want. You are going to take great satisfaction in how well you do, how much work and effort you are putting into things, and what the returns are. Doing these things will give you an extremely satisfying life, and you will be absolutely certain that you are getting the most out of what you've got. You will get much, much further than anyone who started out much better off than you did but didn't expend the effort. This is the sweetest gift of all, watching the underdog (yourself) win and succeed where others fail.

* * *

You should now spend a little time talking about this:

- What do you think about your squiggle?
- What do you think about the initial condition of your boat?
- How do you feel about the fairness or unfairness of life?
- Do you see any improvements your boat could use?
- Do you see how to break a big goal down into bite-sized chunks?
- Do you see how you can view everything you do as getting closer or farther away from your direction in life?

don't believe your own bs!

(How to See What Needs to Be Done)

A big issue in life is figuring out priorities. Priorities are about seeing what needs to be done and *when* it best needs doing. The "when" is a very critical piece to this puzzle. Really seeing what needs to be done (so that you will be able to accomplish any given task) is pretty hard in itself. Figuring out when you should be doing things is usually the killer. Many times, you will find yourself doing the right thing, but doing it at the wrong time, and this always makes the task much harder. If you need to fix the propeller on your boat, you don't start at sunset. Trying to do this in the dark is really hard.

In this section we concentrate on identifying what needs to be done (learning to look for ways to improve your boat and your seamanship) and when the best times are to do it. In the previous section, you should have learned that the key to this is simply having a direction, any direction. Wandering aimlessly through life does not maximize your capabilities, no matter what they are. In figuring out what needs to be done, you have to be very careful not to fall into the trap of believing your own BS.

BEING A GOOD MANAGER

"Don't believe your own BS," is a business phrase (with this and the previous sections, you may be able to tell that I spent considerable time in corporate America). Anyway, the phrase is used as advice for young managers. In order to manage anything (as you should now be thinking about managing your own life, your journey in your little boat), you have to make decisions—should I do this, or should I do that? The best way to make good decisions is to have all the information you need. The accuracy of this information determines the quality of your decision. Yeah, sometimes you might get lucky—the shoot-from-the-hip, cowboy mentality—but if you are gambling your career or your future on the quality of your decisions (and this is truly what life and decision making is all about), you will best be served by getting good at gathering the right information.

Here's where the catch comes in. Management is about making the right decisions, but it's also about the quality of those decisions, performing, doing well, delivering. Businesses are not run like hobbies; they have specific goals. Just like your boat, they have a very specific destination, typically to produce more profit or value than they did for the same period in the previous year. As a result of this single-minded focus (typically everything that the company does is with this goal in mind), managers have to make decisions and then communicate the results to a variety of groups. You have to tell everybody what you're doing and how its going—welcome to Corporate America. You have to tell them how well your decisions turned out.

Everybody is interested in "How's it going?" In a business, everyone cares—the owners, other managers, employees, vendors (people that sell the company products or services), customers, the IRS, and on and on. As a manager of whatever job you have, you are the only one who can really tell everyone else what's going on in your area. No matter how hard you might try not to, it is human nature that you will always put a "spin" on the story of "How's it going?" to make yourself look good. Spin is not necessarily lying, it's just bending the truth to make good stuff seem a little better and bad stuff seem not so bad. This is evidently hardwired into our brains.

You may use a lot of spin or maybe just a little, but it's always there. Senior managers learn to discount anyone's report on "How's it going?" based on how much spin they're used to hearing from that particular manager. This is a Fact of Life— whenever someone asks you "How's it going?" there is spin involved, and not always the same spin to the same people. You may spin more to your employees, or more to your boss, and the spin to the owners is different than the spin to the vendors. Oh, what a tangled web we weave.

The point here is that this just isn't about business, it's about life too! How many times a day do you hear a variation of, "Hey, how's it going?" This, like other stuff in this book, is ingrained into our culture. The ever-present answer to this often-asked question is, "Fine, it's going just fine." SPIN! Is everything *really* ever that fine? This is why there are report cards, information that is hard and fast, with no spin. It's not "soft" information like "good" or "bad" or "fine"—it's a hard number, a 3.1, it's finite, it's your GPA. In business the report cards are called "profit and loss statements." The spin you put on this hard data (especially if it's not so good) is called "excuses," and they might work for a while, but not forever.

FOLLOW THE YELLOW BRICK ROAD

Believing your own spin, especially the excuses, is a huge trap that a lot of people fall into. The theory goes: If you say something often enough, you start to believe it's true, and believing it's true will cause you to make your decisions based on your own spin, your own misinformation. This is spinning out of control. *Don't ever believe your own BS!* You will immediately be able to tell when this is happening the moment you start to feel that everything is OK.

A good way to cut through your own spin, your own BS, is to imagine that you are "working" for yourself. Are you happy with the job that was done or would you fire yourself?

Remember, you are a little boat on a big ocean; NOTHING IS EVER OK, IT'S REALLY DANGEROUS OUT THERE! There's always something that could be done, or done better. So, when you look around and think you are finished with something, anything, you should take the extra moment to really be honest with yourself. Did you do a good job, an acceptable job, or a poor job? After all, it's your own damn boat!

What does all this have to do with managing your own life? It has to do with learning to give yourself a report card, that hard-and-fast data with no spin. Your personal report card should be issued daily, hourly, minute by minute, and the only thing that really matters on it is whether you are getting closer to your goal or farther away—*what direction that decision makes your boat go*. The decision to blow off the book report and watch television gets you farther from your goal if your goal is to be an attorney (because first you have to do well in school to get into law school). Because you were watching an episode of *Law and Order* is just an excuse—it's just spin. Don't believe this BS is helping you toward your goal.

To see better what needs to be done (what you should be doing to improve your boat and your seamanship), you need high quality, accurate information. You will use this information to manage your journey along the path you have chosen in life, whatever path that is. To figure out what information you need, you should first have a very clear idea of what you're trying to accomplish. To save some time here, I'll just flat out tell you that *everyone's job and highest priority should be, first and foremost, managing his or her own life.* You must begin to see yourself in this manner and think about what it means. It's a job. It's work. It's not always fun, but like it or not, as the oatmeal guy says, "It's the right thing to do!" If you start thinking about yourself as your own personal employee, and that employee's job is to manage your life, how simple things become. You can track your performance and give out report cards. Am I getting closer or farther away? Am I doing a good or poor job of managing, making the right decisions more often than bad decisions?

You should have meetings with this employee (just like in business) to ask "How's it going?" Take time every day to review the decisions you made and whether they were good or bad. Be focused with your thinking, not just, "Oh, that was cool, that was a drag." Think about which decisions got you closer to your goal and which ones got you farther away. It's kind of like watching the compass on the boat. If you don't know where you are going, any road will take you there. If you have a goal, a direction, then you can only be doing one of two things, getting closer or farther away. In giving yourself the honest answers to this daily meeting about "How it's going," don't forget that you're the boss! Be critical, be the prosecuting attorney, "Oh yeah, well if it's going so well, how come…" These are hard questions to answer, and it's really not much fun to be on the firing line, but it's well worth the effort.

KNOWLEDGE IS POWER
So when it comes to these "meetings," however unpleasant the news, the only thing that will ever help you to start making the

right decisions is the truth. A great bonus to this review process of taking a quick look at your daily decisions is that by doing so, you notice that your decisions get better. This is how you learn to do better. A life unexamined is not worth living! Your grades will go up, you'll have more time to do what you want, your parents will get off your back, your friends will have more respect for you, and so on. You get all this, but only if you are truthful: "Today was a bad day for decisions, I should have…" As they say at Alcoholic's Anonymous, "The truth will set you free!" Simply hoping for the best is a bad strategy as it seldom, if ever, comes to pass. Ask anyone!

Small Change

I had this girlfriend Loren, and we were really tight, and she was like totally into being with me—hanging out at the movies and doing stuff. Anyway, I was really stupid, and got grounded for a month, no instant messaging, no phone, no going out, no TV. I was really mad, and thought it was like way too much. So, I'm at school the other day and I see Loren, and I ask her what's up, and she doesn't say anything, and I'm all like, "What's going on?" I mean, I'm in all this trouble and can't do anything, and thought that she'd be all on my side and everything, but she was just being all cold.

So I talk to my mom about being grounded, and she starts talking about how hard it is for her, that she didn't ask me to get in trouble, and that it's no fun for her to be grounding me—keeping after me doing my chores, and making sure I'm not cheating on the grounding stuff. I never really thought that this was such a drag for her too, that she was also being kind of grounded for something that I did.

Anyway, I'm at school again, and I see a friend, and he tells me that Loren has been going out with Johnny, and I'm all like, "That bitch!" It really made me think about who you can count on. I was really pissed at my mom and everything, but this was like a big hassle for her, and she was still willing to do all that, to keep me doing the right stuff. Loren, who was supposed to be all into me and everything, just bailed when I really needed her, like when I really needed a payback for all the stuff I'd done for her.

So today, Loren comes up to me and is all sorry and everything, but I just look at her and go, "Whatever!" Everything has a weird way of working out, being unfair, then being kind of fair. You're pretty sure you feel one way about things, and then you find out stuff, and it changes the way you feel.

Max—14

Back to managing your own life. Most people will start from the premise, "OK, this is what I know!" Fair enough, but wrong, wrong, wrong! What you know is part of your own BS. (Remember, this is what you are always trying to convince everyone of, that you know so much!) Come on, you don't know so much, nobody does. Get over it. Even the simplest things have another dimension if you start letting go of the BS that you know so much.

Remember in preschool when you learned what 2 + 2 was? You'd run around telling everybody, like you were so smart. Now you're much older, and knowing that 2 + 2 is 4 doesn't prove so much. You are so certain now that four is the one and only answer. Don't be so certain of so many things. There might be other answers. Two pair is an equally accurate answer to this question. As the questions get tougher in life there are typically many, many right answers. Don't get locked into thinking you've got all of them!

The better strategy is always to start off by trying to identify what you *don't* know. Here's what I'm trying to accomplish. What are things I *should* know in order to be able to accomplish it? Of the things I should know, what is the stuff I don't know, the stuff I'm not so sure about? Once you've identified what you don't know, start figuring out what you need to do to find out.

This will probably be the hardest part of this book for a teenager, and perhaps even harder for parents—learning to admit to the stuff that they don't know or are not sure about. This is always a great place to start when you're trying to figure out what needs to be done, so let's take a really hard look at this mountain of things you don't know.

INFORMATION OVERLOAD

You can look at all the stuff in the world as information. You keep being told you're in the information age, and baby, you are smack dab in the middle of it. You may find yourself needing to know the population of Lima, Peru, or the chemical composition of basalt, or what your girlfriend thought about your date last night. Lots and lots of stuff is sure interesting to know, and indeed, the volume can be quite overwhelming. Information overload is the curse of our era. The Internet and global cable television networks put more information at our fingertips than any humans have ever had available. Instead of being an advantage, I think this is a decided disadvantage. The huge amount of stuff we are being told hides the stuff we *really* need to know. In advertising, we call this "clutter." We have to be very good at dividing up the "need-to-know" stuff from the "nice-to-know" stuff.

Imagine a farmer a thousand years ago—no television, no weather channel, no Internet, pretty much no nothing. This farmer, like his father, and his father's father before him, pretty much had all the information he really *needed* to know in order to survive. Yeah, it would have been nice to know that the Mongol Hordes were about to swoop down on his village, but as the bumper sticker says, "Shit happens." You can't know everything! The point is that this farmer knew from generations of experience what to plant when, what to harvest when, what could kill him, what was safe, and on and on. He had most of the information he "needed" to know. He may have also had a little information about things that were "nice" to know (that God would some day pluck him up into heaven, and he'd finally be away from that horrible farm!). He had an advantage over us because he did not have to deal with a lot of clutter—information that confuses you and causes you to make decisions based on the wrong information. He had simple information and a daily report card of how he was doing. His report card was whether there was food to eat or not. There was very, very little spin in *his* life.

In looking at gathering information about things you don't know, you need to get very good at separating the nice-to-know stuff from the need-to-know stuff. To do this, you need to keep this thousand-year-old farmer in mind. Wherever you plan to end up on your journey, no matter how ambitious it may be, there is someone else who's probably already done it, or has at least done something pretty damn similar. All you have to do is picture these folks in your head, really spend a little time thinking about them—how they live, what they do, all the little stuff that made them what they were. Picture these folks just like that farmer, and think about what they "needed" to know. As I will go into later on, *simply acting the part is perhaps the biggest step in becoming the person you want to be.*

A rookie in the NFL had made his first touchdown catch and began gyrating in the end zone. When he came to the sidelines, the coach whispered in his ear, "Son, try to look like you've been there before!" Looking like you belong is one of the most important types of information you "need" to know. If you really want to get this right, you can get biographies of people you want to be like. Simply copy what they did, how they acted, figure out what information they needed to become what they did. It's really easy and there's no rules or laws against it! Not only do you learn the "what" that these people did, but more importantly, the "when" in their lives they did it.

DON'T KEEP DOING THE SAME THINGS, AND EXPECT DIFFERENT RESULTS

No matter what your present circumstances are (the condition of your boat and your seamanship), you've decided that you really don't know what you want to do, but you have concluded that you would probably be better off with more money than you really need, instead of not having enough. This is a "general" direction that was discussed in Section Three. You don't have to be really specific yet. You're too young to figure everything out, but this is a fairly nonspecific goal, a general direction to move in. Likewise, you could chose to be respected, or to be famous, to be left alone, to be loved, or all of the above.

For this next example, to see what needs to be done and when, let's imagine that having more instead of less money than you need is your general direction. First step: Look at other people (those you know or know about) who are in that boat (having more money than they really need). How do they live? What do they do? What do they know? How do they act? How do they dress? Where do they hang out? How do they talk?

Without being too much of a genius, you can start out by answering these questions for yourself. Better yet, you could spend some time really finding out the real answers to these questions. See, already you are finding things that need to be done and the information you need to know—and once you know it, you can start making those changes in how you live, what you do, what you know, how you act, where you hang out, how you talk, and *when* you should be doing this stuff. This is what I mean about your seamanship.

Once you have a clear picture of how and what you need to be, you can set out on actually being it, and you can concentrate on other information (improvements) you need to acquire. In the example above, if the folks you are trying to emulate have a lot of money, then they must know something about making it, and this is a need-to-know thing. If you want a lot of money, you need to know how to make a lot of money (or how to steal it—a thought I don't recommend). Another thing that they need to know is how to hold onto the money they already have. This too, is a need-to-know thing. I hope you see where I'm going here. As you just keep going down the questioning path, you can get pretty specific. In keeping with the "getting a pile of money" analogy, you can start looking a little harder at other people who have and don't have any money. On the "have" side you've got your doctors and lawyers and brokers (lions and tigers and bears, oh my!) On the "don't have" side, you've got unskilled laborers, the unemployed, and drug addicts. How on earth do you expect to get on the "have" side of this equation when you are dressing, acting, and talking like the "don't have's"!

The One That Got Away

I grew up in the "hood." My hood was in Detroit, and it wasn't the worst part of the ghetto or anything, but it was a very poor, predominantly black neighborhood. I was little when I lived there, but I remember it being pretty rough. We lived with my grandparents while my Dad went to medical school. We weren't starving or anything, but we sure weren't rich either. My granddad still drove the bus, and my grandma worked at a cafeteria.

We moved when I was ten. We moved to Omaha where my Dad and one of his friends from medical school did their internships. Now there are some pretty bad parts of Omaha too, but with what my Dad was making with his internship, what my Mom earned as a legal secretary, and the money they had saved living with my grandparents, we lived in a pretty nice neighborhood. I went to a good school. There were only three other black kids in the school, so I guess I stood out a little. My parents were serious about school work, so I learned to work hard too, and I did pretty well.

Every year during the holidays, we would load up the car and head north to spend Christmas with my grandparents. The thing I really remember are all the kids I grew up with and went to school with. We were all older now, and they were into the whole urban rap, hip-hop thing—the way they talked, and the way they dressed and all that. I guess I had changed in Omaha, because I didn't dress like them anymore, or I guess they really didn't dress like we all used to when we were kids and our moms were buying all our clothes. Anyway, things went on like this, and every time I came back, it was worse and worse. Several of the kids I knew had dropped out of school and were doing and selling all kinds of drugs. We stayed friendly, but we couldn't have been farther apart.

By this time, both my Mom and Dad were doing really well, and we had a big house in the suburbs of Omaha. I was getting ready to go to the university in Lincoln. I felt so bad for the kids I'd left behind. When I'd come back, they still liked me, and I guess deep down, they respected me and were proud of me, kind of like the fish story—the one that got away. They would tell me about all their problems, and of course, want me to get high with them. It was really depressing. What I noticed is that somewhere along the line, we'd stopped speaking the same language. We'd stopped using the same words, stopped pronouncing the words we knew the same way, and spoke of different lives. They wanted to get ahead, to get out too, but they always had a reason why they couldn't, always a reason why it would be tomorrow, always had a reason why they should just sit down and get a little more high.

I told them the truth. I told them they were lazy. I told them they weren't stupid, but they sure as hell were acting stupid. If they wanted something, anything, they would have to work for it. They needed to go back and get their GED, and they needed to stop talking like some bunch of slum trash. They needed to dress better. While they thought they were so cool, and that they could be the next P. Diddy if they just caught a break, it just wasn't going to happen, and nobody was going to hire someone who couldn't speak English. No one wanted someone to be answering their phone by saying, "'sup." They listened, but they didn't hear.

Don't know if I'll ever see those kids again, and I don't know if they ever did anything with what I told them. I start at the University of Nebraska–Lincoln in the fall, and am really looking forward to it. Maybe I'm being sort of a sell out, as they would say, but I'm going to do well and do well for my family, and I'm going to do that by being proud of being black, but also by being proud to be an American—and everything that goes with it.

Thomas–17

Seeing what needs to be done begins with the definition of what you're trying to accomplish, having a direction. The moment you have this direction, you can honestly look at yourself, your condition, and see what information needs to be gathered or what improvements need to be made. As the process starts to unfold, the "when" becomes evident. Say, for whatever reason, you want to be an attorney. Do you start dressing and acting like an attorney in high school? No, that's stupid. You start dressing and acting like a high school student who's going to college because that's the "when" that's in front of you right now. To be an attorney, you have to go to college and graduate, and then go to law school. Maybe this is clearer now, the learning how to think about and see the things that need to be done.

THE TRUTH

Before we move on, we need to touch on a few more points here. Information is king! The more you know, the better off you are. Knowing what you don't know is the first step to finding the truth about anything, but "truth" itself requires a little thought.

From the moment you first go out in the world, you begin your battles with the truth. I'm not talking about the truth you have to tell and then get in trouble for. I'm talking about the real truths of how life is, the information side of truth, what this book is about, the Facts of Life. I'm talking about what information is true and what information is false. This is a big deal because throughout your whole life you are going to have to judge whether certain information is truthful, the whole truth, and nothing but the truth, as they say in the court shows. Since you will be making decisions based on information, and you are going to have to dig this information up, you will quickly find that the truth is not so easy to get a handle on. In fact, if you do your information-digging well, you will find that there are usually several competing and contradictory truths. Pick a subject, a topic, a person, an event, or a situation, and you will find that "the truth" can be pretty elusive. The more important the subject and person, the more spin there will be.

This aspect of "the truth" could be an entire book in itself, but for the time being, I will simply touch on the topics of "Absolute" and "Relative" truths. Absolute truth has no qualifications and is undeniable. Absolute truth is that the Earth is ninety-three million miles from the Sun. Absolute truth is that John F. Kennedy was shot on November 22, 1963. Absolute truth is that this morning, an ounce of gold was worth $352.59. Certain things in life are beyond dispute; they are what they are, they are Absolute. The more you can gather information that contains the Absolute truths, the better off you will be because basing your decisions on relative truths can be extremely dangerous.

Relative truth is that John is your best friend. Relative truth is that you are good at math. Relative truth is that Lee Harvey Oswald assassinated John F. Kennedy. Relative truth is that gold is more valuable than water. Relative truth only makes sense *within a context*, and the moment that context changes, so does the truth. "Context" is an important concept. It's about how things (thoughts, truth, relationships) borrow meaning from their surroundings. Love means one thing with regard to a candy bar, and something else when said on a date. Say you consistently get the highest grades in your algebra class. Within this context, you are good at math, and this statement is the truth. If I take you on a little trip, and we sit down with a group of calculus grad students from Cal Tech, you are no longer very good at math, and this is the truth. Your knowledge has not changed, you have not changed, but the context has.

Since most valuable information is of a Relative nature, you must be able to analyze the context of the truths you are willing to accept and base your decisions on. While you may be a very good football player at your school, it could be a huge error in "believing your own BS" to think that your future holds a Super Bowl ring. It could (virtually everyone who has received a Super Bowl ring played high school football), but here you have to be very careful about the context. How many slots are open in the NFL? How many kids play high school football? Are you not only good in your high school context, but also one of the thousand best in the entire country? Sitting in a restaurant in Manhattan, gold is quite a bit more valuable than water. Sitting in the middle of the Gobi Desert, this may no longer be the case. *Context!*

YOUR BELIEFS, LIKE FINE WINE, WILL ONLY IMPROVE WITH AGE

Decisions are critical to achieving your goals. Accurate information is critical in making the right decisions. Understanding the difference between Absolute and Relative truth is often the difference between your success and failure, whether you are getting closer or farther from your goal. That John is your best friend and has your best interest at heart may be true within the context of this week in school and the fact that you are facing no crisis. Change the context, and the truth may change too. This is another big lesson in the Facts of Life. As you get older, both you and your context will change. This is a given!

What's not so obvious is that as your context changes, so will your truths, what you believe. With this thought clearly in mind, don't be too married to the things you believe today. Expect that the things you believe today will *not* be the things you believe tomorrow!

This works in both general and specific cases. Your truth today might be that the band Slipknot is the most brilliant thing to ever happen to music. I can assure you that your truth will change in less than a decade. If I tell you that one man shot another, and this is all the information you have, you could believe that the first man was wrong to shoot the second. If I then tell you that the second man was a terrorist, you would probably change your belief. The specific information and context has changed your "truth." If I told you that the terrorist became a terrorist because the first man murdered his brothers and sisters, your opinion (your truth) could change again. Always think in terms of the "relativity" of truth (the things you hold most dear) and the need for accurate, absolute information on which to base your decisions. Together, the truth and the context are what help you determine the "when" of what you should be doing, the what needs to be done.

CONTEXT

With respect to this Absolute and Relative nature of truth and information, context becomes the judge and jury. The more you change the circumstances, the more the truth can bend. One of the key issues in thinking about context is considering the context with which you view yourself. Here, once again, it becomes critical to be aware of your own BS, your own beliefs. Here, it's a good idea to take a minute and really think about how you picture yourself (your carefully constructed relative truth) and the absolute truth of who you *really* are. There's a joke I love that not everyone gets. A guy says, "You know, there are two kinds of people in the world, the kind who believe there are two kinds of people in the world…" I know, not a great joke, but it can help you focus on how you see yourself and how others see you. Remember, a big part to getting the role you want in life is to first learn how to play it. If you want to be an attorney, do attorney types of things at the *right* times.

So there is kind of a trick to really seeing yourself, your context, and being as truthful as you can be. The trick is to define yourself just like the dictionary defines words. What would the dictionary say about you? Remember context, not just the context of your group of friends who think you're so cool! What's the absolute and relative truths about you and the way you define yourself. As you think about this, you will find that most of your definitions fall into two categories ("there are two types of people"). Your definitions will be either Consumer based or Producer based.

THE MATERIAL WORLD

As fallible people, we view ourselves as we view our world, and we begin by putting ourselves in one of these two general groups. We either define ourselves as Consumers and judge ourselves based on what we consume (the clothes we wear, the cars we drive, the food we eat) or Producers and judge ourselves based on what we produce (the grades we get, the jobs we have, the skills we've learned, what we are capable of doing). When you view your own personal context through these two lenses, you can come up with two very different pictures.

On your journey through life, you will find that the Producer picture of yourself is always closer to the absolute truth, and that the Consumer picture of yourself is always quite relative. This, too, is a big Life Lesson. Seeing what needs to be done to improve your lot in life (the condition of your boat and your seamanship) is always a Producer-driven equation. The things that matter most are the things you can do. These are the things that really make you who you are. All the other crap is just fluff and can really confuse you in getting an accurate evaluation of who you are, where you're going, and most importantly, what you are going to need to know to get there—the things that need to be done. Clutter, the nice-to-know stuff, is entirely Consumer driven.

You can be anything and get anywhere with the right set of skills, and the right "knowing of what you don't know" gets you off to a fast start. Acting the part is also a big mover in this direction, as long as we don't get caught up in believing our own BS. There's a great Peter Sellers movie about this called *Being There*. The poster for the movie says: "A story about truth, compassion, perception, love, and not incidentally the importance of owning a good suit." You have to see the movie, but the point is that because he looked well off in his nice suit, people thought he was successful and smart.

* * *

Key Points

Priorities, the relative importance of doing one thing or another, seeing *what* needs to be done and *when* it needs to be done, are really important, and this is totally wrapped up with your decision-making process. Making good decisions is all about the accuracy of the information you have on which you base your decisions. These decisions determine your performance, your answer to the ever-present "How's it going?" questions. Cutting through your own spin is essential in dealing with these decisions and your performance, being truthful to yourself, being your own boss, and managing your own life. Be really tough on yourself and know what you don't know. Know what you need to know and know what's just nice to know. Picture people you want to be like and find out about them. Act like them and look like you belong. In going through the process, think in terms of the absolute truth and the relative truth. Think in terms of context, and be able to define yourself with respect to either a consumer or producer type of context. Figure out how you are doing each and every day and give yourself a report card with no spin attached to it.

* * *

You should now spend a little time talking about this:

- What do you think about making decisions and setting priorities?
- What do you think about spin and believing your own BS?
- How do you feel about working for yourself, managing your own life?
- Do you really know how much you don't know?
- What are some nice-to-know and need-to-know kinds of things?
- Who would you like to be like?
- What's an absolute and a relative truth about yourself?
- How do you define yourself as a Producer and as a Consumer?

don't fight the last war!

(How to Find Your Place in the World)

Having a direction in life is a good thing. Learning to find "truthful" information in order to get there is even better. Making the right decisions and reviewing your progress is the best thing. This is pretty simple stuff, but it all has to begin with an accurate idea of where you are. This section will deal with finding your place in the world, the point of departure on your great journey. Say that you want to go from the Atlantic Ocean to the Pacific Ocean through the Panama Canal. What direction would you go? Surprisingly, the answer is not west. The answer is southeast! Look at a map. This is a very good thing to remember because it shows you the importance of knowing where you are in determining which direction you have to go to get to where you want to be. This is called "navigation," and without question, the most important thing in the whole world to a navigator is specifically where they are *right now!*

WAR IS HELL

What on Earth does this have to do with war and fighting? As with the previous sections, the title of this section is a Fact of Life. It's meaning is one of those Absolute truths. This is obviously a military line—"Don't fight the last war!" It means that things change in life and using "out of date" rules to deal with new stuff is a bad, often disastrous strategy. Knowing where you are lets you know which rules you should be applying.

A literal example is found in WWII, so here's a little history lesson. Just before the beginning of the war, Germany was building a ton of weapons and training a very large army. This did not go unnoticed! France, which shares a long border with Germany, was particularly concerned. They looked at their relatively recent experience in WWI to come up with a solution (using "out of date" rules). Since WWI was a very messy, nasty war fought over several years with complex trenches used to fortify static front lines, the French generals assumed things would be pretty much the same and built what came to be known as the Maginot Line along their border with Germany. This defensive system consisted of a series of trenches and fortifications similar to those used in WWI. This too, did not go unnoticed. The French did a very good job building these defenses. They were massive, formidable, and very well equipped. The Germans sure would have a hard time getting through this great barrier!

Unfortunately for the French, the Germans also remembered WWI and realized that going head to head against these defenses was not a very smart move. They figured out that with changing circumstances (the advent of airplanes and motorized tanks and vehicles), they should use new rules of engagement. When they finally attacked, they drove into Belgium, a very small and undefended country just north of France. The Germans blew through Belgium and northern France so quickly that their biggest problem was supplying themselves with enough fuel to keep moving so fast. (The entire French army was waiting on the Maginot Line.) By the time the French realized what was going on and retreated to Paris (in order to defend their capitol), the Germans were already there. France fell, and the French learned a big lesson about fighting the last war. America had a similar experience in Vietnam. There have been a lot of similar examples throughout history where the folks in charge used out-of-date rules to face new circumstances.

LIVING LIFE FORWARD

The Life Lesson here is that great danger inherently exists in relying totally on the rules and practices of the past to face the future. This doesn't mean we should ignore the past or those experiences, because they *are* hugely important. It means we should view the past and those experiences in *context*—that is, when these events happened and what was going on when they occurred. The past has a lot of relevance for sure, but it does not necessarily apply to today. You have to learn to *adapt* that past experience to the challenges that face you today. This is about knowing where you were, where you are, and which rules apply.

Killing Time

You could be kind of a geek in middle school, and it was no big deal. I mean, you're kind of just a kid, and you can be sort of stupid like a kid, and nobody really cares. When I went to Shorecliff's, I pretty much hung out with the kids I knew from elementary school, the kids that I knew from the neighborhood. Anyway, I'm in high school now. Two of my friends that I grew up with, Chad and Daryll, had older brothers, and when high school started, they were kind of cool because everybody knew their brothers and everything. They started hanging out with this group of sophomores, and we were still kind of friends, because we'd done a bunch of stuff together and everything, but I started to hang out with some other kids that were in my classes.

So one day, it wasn't that long after school started, and I was hanging out, and I saw Chad and Daryll talking with their group and standing around and stuff. We used to go to this old construction site down the hill from where we lived and play this game we came up with that was kind of like tag and kind of like hide-and-seek. We called it hunt-and-seek, because you didn't really do that much hiding. Anyway, a bunch of kids from the neighborhood would play and it was pretty fun, kind of something to do after school and everything. I'd talked to some of the other guys that played, guys I still hung out with, and we were trying to get a big group together to play because the more people who played, the more fun it was.

So, I really wasn't doing anything and saw Chad and Daryll and everything, and really didn't think about it too much, just went up to them and asked if they wanted to play hunt-and-seek after school that day. I walked up and said hey, and they said hey, and then I asked them, and they looked at me, and everybody was looking at me, and they all started to laugh. Chad said he didn't think he'd be playing hunt-and-seek very much anymore, and everybody laughed again, like I was so stupid or something, and they were so cool.

I just said, "whatever," and walked away, and thought they were being assholes. I mean, it's just something to do after school, and we used to do it all the time, but they just made me feel like a jerk, and like they were too cool for school and everything.

I saw my other friends and told them that I just wasn't into it anymore, and we just went over to Rob's house after school and sat around. We really didn't talk about it, but I thought it was pretty stupid, that like we were too old or something to have fun. It was like a week later, and we got a game together, not with Chad or Daryll or anything, and it just wasn't fun. It was like it could have been fun, but I guess from what they said and everything, I felt kind of stupid. We never played hunt-and-seek again, and just spent more time kind of sitting around talking. I guess that's what you're supposed to do when you get older or something, but I really miss all the fun we used to have running around that construction site. We'd be screaming and running, and making fun of each other, but I guess that's just kid stuff now.

Alex—16

With growing up and getting older, you face a series of steps that require you to change your rules. These are the rules of how you behave, how you act. Back in elementary school, probably around first or second grade, if a boy had a crush on a girl, either he was so shy that he did nothing about it, or if he wasn't so shy, he would probably be mean to that girl—push her, taunt her, put her proverbial pigtails in the inkwell. In the twisted psychology of a first grader, this is the result of having feelings for her, while trying to find an "acceptable" way of interacting that doesn't invite the wrath of his peers. ("Johnny's got a girl friend, Johnny's got a girl friend.") This works in first grade. Now let's step ahead to high school, and the same boy has a crush on a different girl. Here, many boys try the same technique (with perhaps a little more subtlety, but still the same out-of-date, mean-to-her rules). This behavior doesn't work so well in high school. This is an example of "fighting the last war." This is using outdated "rules of engagement."

When you look at it this way, it is pretty easy to see how inappropriate the old behavior is in the new circumstance. This is what people mean when they talk about maturity. It's using the appropriate rules at the appropriate time—swearing in front of your friends to be "cool," but not swearing in front of adults. Understanding this is a big step, the first step, in finding your place in the world. There's a great line that was almost the title of this section, "When in Rome, do as the Romans do." It is a very old line. It's proof that this stuff is a Fact of Life and pretty much always has been. It's not a matter so much of "where" you are as "when" you are. If you're in high school, are you at the beginning of this stage, the middle, or the end? What set of "rules of engagement" are you using? Think about all the areas of your life where you may be using out-of-date rules of engagement—whining to get your way, crocodile tears, bullying, throwing a fit, or waiting for mommy and daddy to bail you out of trouble. "You're acting like a baby!" The active word here is "acting." You need to act like who you want to be, and a big part of this acting involves your ability to show that you understand the new rules of behavior by using them. "If you want to be treated like an adult, then act like one!" This is all a lesson in understanding how things change and accepting it. It's all about seeing yourself move through time, knowing where you are in the process.

A person's World View has to change with the changing stages of life. The relative truths (the rules that work) have changed because the context (the world you live in) has changed. This is why you shouldn't fight the last war—you will probably end up speaking German! These rules are complicated and confusing for kids. One of the hardest things for kids to understand is that their rules (what's OK and what isn't) are not the same as the rules for their younger or older brothers and sisters. What's OK for a 12 year old may not be for a 16 year old. Parents get this. Kids don't!

AGES AND STAGES

You go through different stages in life and you're a different age as you do. This may seem like the same thing, but it's not. Your world changes and so do you. The problem is that these stages and ages don't always happen at the same speed. Just like growing up (physically getting larger), sometimes you go through a "maturity spurt," like a "growth spurt." You're moving and so is the target (what you should be accomplishing in each stage of your life). It's like trying to change a tire on a moving car. Knowing that both you and the target are moving gives you a very different kind of navigation problem than if you were just standing still. It's one thing to be motionless and think of a direction to go. It's something entirely different when you're moving because you now have to choose both the direction and the "when."

For example, if you are in Denver and want to go to San Francisco, you need to go west. If you are flying from Denver to Seattle, the direction of San Francisco changes every minute you're on the plane. By the time you get to Seattle, San Francisco is south. Going from middle school to high school is one issue, but your level of maturity as you do it creates this "direction of San Francisco" problem. If you've completed and remember all the middle school Life Lessons, it's a piece of cake, and the "when" of moving on to high school is on track. If you haven't, you will have problems figuring out the new rules of engagement and the direction you should be going because you still have to achieve that middle school level of maturity before you attempt the high school stuff. It's the same as you move from high school to college, or college to working, or single to married, and so on.

So you should be thinking about your understanding of the stage you are in and where you are in maturity to deal with it. It's about the level of someone's maturity as they face the challenges of the world they're living in at the time. The "world" you live in is defined by the stage of life. The world of an elementary school student is quite different from the world of a college student.

Back to the Maginot Line. The French generals were very old. They got very good at believing their own BS, and as a result, they kept the same rules in place for conducting the pending "new" war. As you get older, and the more successful you think you have been, the more you become convinced that you not only *know* what you are doing, but that you also *knew* what you were doing in the past. This is probably the biggest problem with getting older, the thinking that you've got it down. Anyway, many of the German generals were young. The young German generals had no set way of thinking. If the old French generals thought about it, they would have probably taken a harder look at the younger German generals. They would have seen that everything the Germans were building and training for involved speed. Understanding this, they would have probably taken a second look at their Maginot Line. Knowing about the existence of new rules and new ways of looking at things will keep you from thinking you know what you're doing. Don't think you always know so much.

PASSING GO, COLLECTING $200

Finding your place in the world, at least as it relates to the Facts of Life, is all about realizing you are in a certain stage that has certain rules of engagement, and that you are at a certain maturity level in this stage. This is what I mean by finding your place in the world. In high school, you are supposed to learn about "multitasking," keeping several balls in the air at the same time like a juggler. Your level of maturity, your ability to act your age is all determined by how well you are doing with this multitasking. Really being honest with yourself, looking at your life this way, you should be able to clearly see the direction you need to go. You should be able to see the things you need to do in order to become more adept at multitasking, thereby timing things so that you complete your maturity level as you complete the stage.

You may have some catching up to do, or you may be able to coast a little. You have four years in high school. If, by the end of these four years, you don't learn to become good at managing several different things at the same time, you are not ready for the next stage, and are giving yourself a huge handicap. You are falling behind, and it's much harder to catch up than it is to stay ahead. This is about fine tuning your seven or eight inches. Not fighting the last war is as much about getting ready for the new rules as it is abandoning the out-of-date ones. You have to be doing the right stuff at the right time so that you're ready for the next challenge, and the new rules that need to be learned. Life is constantly in motion.

Finding your place in the world, really knowing where you are, involves taking a very hard look at the stage of life you are in, avoiding the rules from the previous stage (at least those that don't apply) and getting ready for the next stage. This means, for you as a teenager, that you need to alter your middle school behavior to fit the multitasking requirements of high school, while getting ready for the more "adult" kind of rules that will be required when you graduate. These "adult rules" include: being responsible and forthcoming for your actions, accepting blame, putting other people's needs before your own, supporting yourself, doing what you have to do before you do what you want to do, and being responsible—all the "not fun" stuff adults have to do.

Finding your place in the world is mostly about this "when" of things—the "when" you are (how old, how mature you are), the "when" of your stage, and the "whens" of your last and upcoming stages. It is also about the size of the world you operate in, its physical dimensions.

MORE ABOUT CONTEXT

To really bring this home, we need to take a close look at these *worlds* we operate in, and the *context* we find in those worlds. Context refers to the situations you can expect to face and the appropriate rules that allow you to face them. You start life with a trip home from the hospital. Yeee haw, here we go! For the first couple of months of your life, even though you are not very conscious of it, your entire world is limited pretty much to the sides of your crib. You're not very aware of all the stuff that goes on outside the bars of your crib. You can think of your world in terms of physical boundaries.

As you get a little older, you become a little more mobile, and gravity ceases to be your worst enemy. You start to move around. Your world gets bigger; it's now about the size of the interior of wherever you are living at the time (barring any baby-gates and the like). Once we've had this taste of freedom, this bigger world, we don't want to go back to the older, smaller world we came from. Watch a baby being put back in their crib. Unless they are exhausted, there's typically a lot of screaming going on. We hate going back! This is a good Life Lesson in itself. Everybody likes moving into a bigger world, but usually never the reverse.

After a while, you begin to walk, and your world expands again. You are now being introduced to the great outdoors, and your world now becomes the size of your house and your yard, or maybe even your neighborhood. Now we scream and yell when it's time to come in. Big moments in anyone's life are the moments when their world changes size. We tend to think that it's the *event* that's so exciting, but it's really about being confronted with a whole lot of new, unexplored territory.

Every time your world changes in size there is a new set of rules and practices that need to be learned in order to deal with it. Going to kindergarten is a BIG moment in the life of a kindergartner because this is the biggest leap they have experienced in the size of their world so far. Their world is now as big as the distance from the house to the kindergarten classroom. There are kids there from other neighborhoods and strange adults wandering around. As you get good at dealing with this bigger world, you think *you* are getting pretty big too! Don't confuse your own size with the size of the world you are living in. You need to always be thinking that there are both bigger and smaller worlds out there. It's a common mistake to not realize that you are only "big" in a "small" world. This is the first lesson in learning about context. You may be a big shot for a kindergartner, but that's it. You are not such a big shot to elementary school kids, you are smaller yet to middle school kids, and tiny to kids in high school. Even in high school, there are many levels of bigger worlds ahead of you. Always remember, you're never as "big" as you think!

WORLDS OF INFLUENCE

It's interesting that our society has created a fairly complicated system for gradually introducing children to an ever-expanding "world of influence." The bigger the world you are involved in, the more its influences affect you. A bigger world has more influence on you, and you should have more influence on it. It's the fish in the pond story, the big fish in a little pond, or as the case may be, a little fish in a little pond. Your pond is the stage of life you are in and your "size" has to do with your maturity in that pond. No matter how big you get in that pond, be prepared to be a little fish in the next pond, and remember that people in the bigger ponds will never see you as the size you see yourself.

So going to kindergarten is a big deal, and then going to first grade is another big deal because now the world is as big as the elementary school, with kids from six to ten or eleven years old. We cool our jets for a few years in a world this size and absorb its lessons, then move to middle school. Here we start to have different teachers for different subjects, and we begin going out in the world with only our friends (to the movies, the mall, the beach). Our physical world is getting bigger and the rules of behavior are changing. In high school we begin to drive cars. This is a huge deal because being able to drive radically increases the size of the world you operate in. The next jump is usually going away to college.

Eventually, if you choose to, you can operate in the "global village." As an international businessperson, diplomat, or politician, you can influence and be influenced by the whole world. Very few people get this "big." People like George Bush, Nelson Mandela, and Bill Gates live in this global world, but there are many, many worlds for adults. There are worlds for doctors and lawyers and clergy and politicians, and worlds for bar flies and drug addicts and criminals. You can imagine how these "spheres of influence" work. A lawyer may be a big shot in the courtroom, but is not so important when wheeled into an emergency room.

South of the Border

I grew up in Mexico City where my father was an attorney for an oil company. We moved to the U.S. when I was 13 years old because he had a very big opportunity with an American oil company. In Mexico City, I went to a private school, and the work was a little more than hard. I did well, and was very proud of my achievements and my family. We lived in a big house and had a lot of prestige. Once, the mayor of the city had dinner with our family. It was a big event. When we moved, I was excited about America, and all the things we were going to do there.

Finally, the day came, and we flew to Los Angeles where my father would be working. I thought Los Angeles would be beautiful, the city of angels, but when we got there, I was disappointed. There are parts that are very, very nice, and there are parts that are very, very poor, but overall, I thought that Los Angeles had no soul, kind of a funny thing for the city of the angels.

Once we were settled in, I started school, and little did I realize what an education I was going to get! I had studied English in Mexico, and was one of the best students in my class. Both my parents spoke English because of their jobs, and once a week at home, we would practice at dinner, speaking only English during the whole meal. This was always fun.

When I started school in America, I thought I would make many friends because I always had many friends in Mexico and I liked being smart and popular. I found this to be a false hope once I arrived. It seems that although I thought I spoke excellent English, it wasn't so. I was proud to be Mexican, but here, the word itself was demeaning! The other kids started by making fun of my accent, or when I would mispronounce something, or use the wrong word. This made me angry, but what was worse was that I could tell they thought I was stupid. They thought I was stupid because this was a second language for me. I'd like to see how well they did trying to speak Spanish or go to school in a foreign country.

Anyway, the white kids were pretty mean to me. There were quite a few Hispanic kids who spoke Spanish, and most of these were second or third generation here in America. They were tough kids, and they didn't mix very much with the white kids. When I would talk to them, even though we were speaking Spanish, it was a different Spanish, and although they didn't think I was stupid, they thought I was trying to be better than them, and this was harder than putting up with the white kids.

Mexico is a much more class-conscious country than America, and because of how I grew up there, I was not the same as the kids whose parents had emigrated years ago. So, the great move that I thought would be so exciting was not. One group was unfriendly because they thought I was stupid and had an accent, and another was unfriendly because they thought I was trying to be better than them. I was so unhappy. I spent long hours doing my school work and stayed in my room a lot listening to talk radio shows so that I could practice losing my accent. It was a very lonely time for me. To make it worse, our house was so much smaller. I felt poor and alone.

Time passed, and I did make friends, fiends from both groups. I guess my white friends were not so concerned about how smart I was, and my Hispanic friends didn't think I was trying to be any better than them. We all grew up some, but I'll never forget that feeling I had. Every time I see someone struggling with their English, wherever they're from, I think about how I felt, and my heart goes out to them.

I wish I could find it in me to yell at the nasty white kids who thought they were so superior—yell at them and say, you think you're so smart and so much better, well the lowly maid in your house speaks English, and you're too stupid to learn Spanish! Who is better than whom?

Carlos—18

So there are many, many worlds out there, and you can choose which ones you'll live in, but for now, you're still in high school. I mention this stuff as part of the process, part of finding your place in whatever world you're in at the time, and seeing the worlds you might operate in as you get older. You need to be figuring out which world you are looking at to find your place, and what the rules and challenges of that world are. So, let's take a closer look at the high-school-sized world and its challenges.

THE FASTER I GO, THE BEHINDER I GET

Here you need to be a good thinker because the challenges are maybe not what you think they are. This is the counterintuitive part. You might think that high school is about world history, science, algebra, football, drill teams, and the prom. It is all about this stuff to some degree, but this stuff is really only there to test you. It's not really about algebra or geometry. You're right when you think that you will probably never use this information again in your life! This is not need-to-know stuff, just nice-to-know stuff.

What high school is really about is sifting out the riffraff. What I'm saying here is that throughout your life, very few people are really going to care whether you know the date that the Magna Carta was signed, but the grades you receive and your ability to absorb certain things and then report those things back *is* a big deal. This is an indication of how good you are at adapting to new rules and new information—the world uses this as a yardstick to measure you and the doors that will be open to you in the future. High school is about testing your ability to learn new rules just for the sake of doing it. It's also about juggling several things at once.

The thing you should be learning here is "multitasking." You have several different classes with different teachers and students in all those classes. You have sports teams, and clubs, and music and cheerleading, and your oh-so-important social life. Are you capable of juggling all these balls at once—and succeeding? The classes and stuff are just practice obstacles to get you ready for real life, where the real obstacles are making a living, supporting a family, being responsible in your community, paying taxes, and on and on. When you try to excuse your poor performance in a class or activity by minimizing the need for that particular information, you are missing the whole point. It's not about knowing algebra or being on the soccer team—it's about meeting that challenge, learning a subject just for the sake of proving that you can do it. Once you have, you can move on to the next stage. If you can't, you get stuck—you don't pass "go" and you don't collect $200.

School is just a big competition, a test, and the subject matter is not as important as many of the other lessons you should be learning. The subject matter is mostly there so that you can practice learning new stuff and demonstrate how good you are at learning it. Those who can't or are too lazy are eliminated from the race. All the kids who understand this are thrilled when they see someone being lazy or "too cool for school." The sharp students learn to cheer for the demise of one more competitor, one more kid who won't be competing with them for college, for jobs, for the satisfaction they are trying to get out of life. The kids who are eliminated are stuck reliving their high school years like Al Bundy in the TV show *Married with Children*.

WHERE'S WALDO?

Finding out and really knowing where you are in the world so that you can navigate to where you want to be is a matter of truly knowing yourself. Where are you in the stage you're in? Where are you in your own maturity? What's the size of the pond you are coming from? Don't try to be something you're not. Accept the reality of your shortcomings and your strengths. You probably have some real catching up to do. You have time. The race isn't over yet, but start getting your act together and think about where you're going!

If you are a 16-year-old junior in a high school in Nebraska, you are more than halfway through the high school stage. You are maybe a little immature for where you should be (you are a "young" junior, most juniors are 17), and the high school in Nebraska is a relatively small world (kind of an isolated, small pond). If you are a 19-year-old senior in a high school in Manhattan, you are almost done with the high school stage. You should be more mature than your classmates and high school in Manhattan is a pretty big pond. Be aware of what you've been exposed to and what you haven't (kind of like knowing what you don't know). Also, I mentioned a 16-year-old junior as maybe being a little immature, but remember, an 18-year-old junior could also be just as immature. It's not how many birthdays you've had, but where you really *are* that matters.

Knowing exactly where you are will keep you from making more than your fair share of mistakes. For example, let's suppose the two fictional kids described above end up at Notre Dame. (Good for them, a very good school!) The first kid will be jumping into a larger pond (Nebraska to Indiana), while the second kid will be jumping to a much smaller pond (New York to Indiana). Both these changes will require them to adapt in different ways, and knowing precisely where they are coming from will help them be successful in this new environment by not applying their out-of-date rules of engagement, not fighting the last war.

Neither behaviors from Nebraska or Manhattan are necessarily appropriate to South Bend, the town where the Notre Dame campus is located. It's all about being honest about your background, the condition of your boat. You shouldn't discount or overemphasize any advantages or disadvantages you have had so far. You should simply be the person you are, coming from the place you've been and going to the place you're going. Accept the changing nature of things and how you are changing to meet the challenges in front of you.

Well, this is a whole lot of information about stages and ages. Remember that fish are seldom aware of the water they swim in. Likewise, most people are not really thinking about the stages of life they are in. Knowing you're in a stage is one thing; figuring out what you're supposed to be getting out of it is entirely different. Are you getting the stuff (knowledge, information, life lessons) you should?

❊ ❊ ❊

Key Points

You need to know where you are starting from to figure out the things you need to do to get to where you want to go. You need to navigate, to understand that there are sets of rules attached to certain worlds you operate in. You need to be aware of the new rules, get prepared for them, and abandon the old, out-of-date rules that no longer apply. You need to think about whether you are using old rules to face the future, the context of the stage of life you are in. Maturity is all about your use of the right rules at the right time. It's about how you act, and it works the same way as physically growing up.

Most importantly, you need to concentrate on understanding the lessons you should be learning during each stage of your life and trying to learn them by the time that stage is finished. You need to really be honest with yourself about the size of the world you are operating in and your size within it. It's like the fish in the pond. You need to think about the world you are operating in, it's influence on you, and your influence on it. You have to measure your ability to adapt to the new rules of engagement you are faced with. You should be thinking about each stage, completing the one you're in while getting ready for the next.

✳ ✳ ✳

You should now spend a little time talking about this:

• What do you think about the rules of engagement for various stages of life?

- What do you think about the changing rules of behavior?
- How do you feel about your own maturity and where you should be?
- Do you see your next stage and do you have any idea what its rules are going to be?
- Do you understand the size of the world you operate in and its relationship to other worlds?
- Do you realize the lessons you should be learning in the stage you're in?

someone always has a bigger boat!

(How to Be Rich)

This section is a lot about math. It's about money, and money is a lot about math. It's kind of long, but there's a lot to be said about money. It might not be a bad idea to get a calculator out so you can walk through some of the examples yourself. It might not be a bad idea to learn as much as you can about math because it's really helpful when dealing with money. Understanding the way percentages work is crucial to understanding taxes and interest, two really big items when it comes to money. This section will try to help you understand money—how it works, what it really is, and how to get your hands on it.

THE BEST THINGS IN LIFE AREN'T FREE!

Knowing that someone always has a bigger boat is a rich person's Fact of Life. You may not really think about it this way, but the rich understand that money is relative. In other words, *the value of money is completely meaningless unless you have something you need to do with it.* Its value is attached to whatever world you happen to live in, whatever needs you might have. Although $1,000 is a finite thing, it has a very different "meaning" for an investment banker than it does for a high school student—it means a little to one and a lot to another. So the first really big thing to know about money is that it is only really meaningful when you don't have enough. Have you ever heard of someone who had too much money? This should be obvious, but the point here is that if you *know* you are going to need it, why on Earth don't you *plan* for it?

Carpe Diem

Taylor and me worked at Cold Stone's. It's an ice cream place. We both got our driving permits and were trying to save some money to get cars. Taylor's parents told her that they would help her out, that they would match whatever she was able to save. I told my parents, and they said that they'd do the same thing with me. We were so pumped and had all these plans. We didn't make much money at Cold Stone's, but we both already had some money saved, and all we figured we'd really need was about a thousand dollars, like you could get a pretty good used car for two thousand, so we both needed about another six hundred dollars or so. We both said that we'd put away $25 a week so that by the time we got our real licenses, we'd have the money to get cars.

For the first couple of weeks, we were still pumped, and it was like really easy to save the money. The spring formal was coming up and I wanted to get this dress I saw. Taylor wanted one too! It was pretty expensive, and my Mom said she'd pay half, just like the car. Taylor's Mom said "no way" to her.

Anyway, I had like a bunch of money, and got $50 to pay for the dress. Taylor's Mom had this dress she said she could wear, and it was kind of cool, but kind of old. We went to the formal and it was really fun. I could tell that Taylor was kind of bummed about her dress and everything, but when we got there, we were just hanging out and dancing and it wasn't really a big deal anymore. Taylor's really pretty, and her Mom's dress looked good. Anyway, we went, and then it was just kind of back to school, and back to working at Cold Stone's and trying to save for the cars. A month or two went by and we were still saving money and everything, but some other stuff came up, and I spent some more money on stuff I needed, but was still saving some of what I got. Pretty soon, summer was coming up, and Taylor was almost done saving her money, she only needed like $75 more, and she'd have the thousand. I needed like another $300, and even though I could still have my parents match the $700 I had, you don't really get much for $1,500. I was kind of bummed, and Taylor started going with her Dad to look at cars and stuff, and I guess I was kind of jealous of her.

Anyway, another friend, Julie, was going with her parents to Hawaii for two weeks, and they said I could go if I could get my own plane ticket. The ticket was about $250, and I had $700, and it wasn't like I was going to get a car right away anyway, so I got the ticket and went with Julie to Hawaii. It was really fun, but it went by really fast. I got home, and Taylor had got this older Honda that was really cute. She also was applying for this other job, because she had a car to get there and everything. Taylor got her car, and she got this other job, too, that paid like twice what we were getting at Cold Stone's.

The summer went by, and I didn't really save any more money because there was always other stuff I needed to get. I still have about $500, but I don't have a car. I've got that dress, but I don't really know when I'll wear it again, and Hawaii was pretty cool, but I'd rather have a car now. I'm proud of Taylor, that she had a plan and everything, and stuck with it, and now has the car, and can pay for her insurance and gas and stuff, and she still has more money than me because of her new job. Anyway, we're still really good friends and she gives me lots of rides and everything.

Blair—17

Money is all about "relativity." Everett Dirkson, a U.S. Senator, once said, "a billion here, a billion there, and pretty soon, you're talking 'real' money!" No matter what you want to accomplish in life, you can count on needing a certain amount of cash (very few lifestyles require no money at all). If you'd like to live in the world of Manhattan socialites, you can count on needing a lot of money. If you want to live in the world of religious missionaries, you will probably only need enough to get there. The first lesson to understanding money is that you are going to need it in the future, you can count on it! The second lesson is that, knowing you'll need money in the future, you should *plan ahead* so that you have the money you can expect to need. Money is very hard to get quickly! It takes time to make money!

Your general direction in life, what it is you would like to accomplish, will determine both the amount of money you are going to need and its relative value. You need to think about money this way instead of blindly trying to get your hands on it and then trying to figure out what you want to do with it. Money is too precious (too hard to get your hands on) to be careless with. It represents big chunks of your time and effort. When it comes to money, you need to really see The Big Picture—not only what you think you might need next week, but what you need next *month*, next *year*, and in the next *decade*. You need a plan, and this should be a very long-range plan that takes care of both next year *and* next week!

GOOD INTENTIONS DON'T PAY THE RENT

A money plan is called a "budget." If money is like a nail, then your budget (your long-range plan) is like a hammer. It puts the nail where you want it. The nail is pretty useless without the hammer and vice versa. Without a plan, without trying to anticipate what you are going to need in the future, you will find that you *never* have enough money. (You spent $30 on a guitar tuner without thinking that you would need to buy tickets to next Friday's dance.) This road is full of regrets. Once money is gone, you can't get it back—you need new money. If the guitar tuner is worth more to you than the dance (relativity), you did the right thing, and this should be part of your plan. If the dance was more important, you screwed up by not thinking ahead. This holds as true for next week's dance as it does for needing a car next year, needing a house when you get married, needing insurance when you get hurt or sick, and on and on. These are all things that are on the horizon for you.

I mentioned before that your number-one job is to manage your life, and one of the biggest things you can successfully manage about your life is your money. You need to start immediately. Starting early makes a huge difference, as we'll see later. No matter how much or how little you may have, you need to manage it. In fact, the less you have, the more carefully you need to manage it! You are probably thinking that budgets, plans, and investments are only for rich people, but the truth is that these budgets, plans, and investments are how they became rich people in the first place.

You're probably thinking that this doesn't sound like any fun at all! It really isn't! Money is hard work. Get this through your head! "Budget" is a bad word. It's one of those words with a lot of spin attached to it. ("I'm on a budget (big frown face)." "The budget seats were horrible!") The word "budget" has gotten itself all wrapped up with the word "cheap," and this is a word with even worse spin. In your mind, "budget" is tied to all the things you *can't* do instead of the things you really *want* to do. "Budget" should not be a bad word. It should be very positive if you look at it as a way to get what you want. A budget will get you whatever you want, guaranteed, every time! This is the huge "secret" to money—you can have all you want, you just need the right plan!

BABY STEPS

The only use for money is to get you things, just like a car gets you where you want to go. The lack of money, like the lack of a car, keeps you from doing things (this includes "just" surviving). What may not be so obvious is that you need to be thinking about your goals and not about the money. If you become very goal- and budget-oriented, you will instantly become "rich" because, all of the sudden, you will find that you always have enough money for what you want to do. This is the definition of being "rich"—always having enough! The catch is that to start the process, you need to wait for a while, and this should be the first part of your plan or your budget. You are going to need to wait and let your "wealth" build up a little. You will need to start the planning process with some amount of savings. Think about savings as the gas tank in your car. It's a hell of a lot easier and more comfortable to have a full tank and add gas as you go instead of always running on fumes. There's also the concept of the "war chest." When kings would go to war, they would start by getting as much dough together as they could and stashing it in their war chest. They didn't want to get halfway through the war and run out of money to pay their soldiers—a sure way to lose a war. In this respect, life is a lot like a war.

You have to start your plan by saving long enough to accumulate a little wealth. This money should be enough to maintain your budget or your plan—it's the initial amount of "gas" in your gas tank. Money will be coming in and money will be going out of your budget and your pocket—daily! This is called "cash flow." Cash flow is how your plan should work. How much do I have right now, how much can I expect to come in over the next week, month, year, and so on, and how much will be going out? Over time, just like gas in the gas tank, money goes in and gets used up.

Now this is important: *Write your plan down!* Really! You need to do this so that you can see how you're doing in the future. In a week or a month, figure out where you are with respect to where you thought you'd be. As you do so, you can make changes, and your plan will get better and better. With practice, everything you do gets better, and I would hope that you would want to have the best money plan you could possibly have! Using your plan makes it better, so the sooner you start, the better you'll be when the money starts to get significant! Planning is important when you make $10,000 a year, and even more important in the future when you make $100,000 a year!

Your plan (budget) should have columns for weeks or months or even days. For each column, you should start with the first line: "Beginning Balance." This is the total of everything you have at the beginning of the period—what you start with. The next line should be "Additions." Here you list all the amounts you expect to come in during the period. After this, you have "Depletions." This is the list of all the amounts that you plan on spending. The last line is "Ending Balance." This is the sum of your Beginning Balance and Additions minus Depletions. The Ending Balance is equal to the next period's Beginning Balance.

Example of a Weekly Budget

Week Ending	2/14	2/21	etc.
Beginning Balance	$40.00	$45.00	$25.00
Additions			
Allowance	$10.00	$10.00	
Yard Work	$15.00	$15.00	
Birthday	$50.00		
Depletions			
Movies	$15.00	$10.00	
Video Game	$45.00		
Poster	$10.00		
Skateboard Deck		$35.00	
Ending Balance	$45.00	$25.00	

HEALTHY, WEALTHY, AND WISE

The plan is all about *spending* and *earning* money over time. Both are equally important to manage, but I am not going to dwell on the spending side very much. How you spend your money has to do with your own personal goals and values. It's *your* money. Just pay attention to where it goes and check to see that this is where you really want to spend it. Are you using the hammer to put the nails where you want them? Know that for every *dollar* you spend, you will need to earn almost *two dollars*. So don't think about it as a $150 skateboard—think about it as having to earn $300 to get the skateboard. I'll explain this later in detail. Making a budget and paying attention to it is work, and it takes time and effort. You may think that you can keep it all in your head, but you would be surprised at how forgetful we can be. Do the work. Write it down. The most critical part of your budget is comparing your "projections" (what you thought was going to happen in the future) to "actual" (what really did happen). You were expecting $15 from yard work, but it rained and you didn't get it. This throws your budget off. Compare "actual" to "projected" at the end of each period and make changes going forward. Concentrate more on the earning side of the equation because it is the hardest to control.

So back to money in general. Money represents "energy" over a period of time, as if that money is frozen energy! This is the Value of Energy concept. The "energy value" for a day laborer is about $7 per hour. The energy value for a neurosurgeon is about $5,000 per hour. The energy value of a manufacturing plant might be $50,000 per hour. For a $100,000, you could "buy" two hours of the manufacturing plant's time, 20 hours of the neurosurgeon's time, or 14,268 hours of the day laborer's time (that's seven years, by the way, at forty hours per week). It's all interchangeable and, as you can see, changes dramatically. Because you only have a limited amount of time (your individual seven or eight inches), you need to pay attention to the specific value you get for your energy.

Money is the universal measurement for equating the value of one type of energy for another. This is about the value of your time and energy versus the value of the time and energy it takes to put a gallon of milk on a shelf in the grocery store. You can't control how much that milk costs; you can only control how much you make and how much time it will take you to make it.

High Noon

Awhile back everybody around where I lived kind of got into paintballing. I mean, like mostly the kids, but some parents too! You use paintball guns and go to these places where they make it like a war zone. They divide you up into two teams and you shoot at each other. If you get hit, the paintball splatters, and you're out of the game. There's a referee and everything. I got to go for the first time and it was kind of scary. I didn't want to get shot because it looked like it hurt. I saw some guys that had these big welts where they got hit. Anyway, you've got to wear all this stuff for protection, a helmet with a visor and sweatshirts. So I went, and you can rent all this stuff, which is pretty cool, but the guns they give you are pretty crappy. They don't shoot very far and they're slow. Most of the guys out there have their own stuff, and they've got these guns that are really fast, and have a lot of pressure. They're like these paintball machine guns.

So we're running around, trying not to get shot, and I see these guys from the other team and I start to shoot. It's like plunk…plunk…plunk…and the paintballs just kind of fly off. They're not very accurate. They see me, and there's just like a thousand paintballs flying all around me, and I get hit right in the visor, and I was out—you have to go out of the game when you get hit. It was really unfair because they could shoot so much faster.

Anyway, it was fun, but when we left, we were all talking about getting our own stuff that was high-end so we could have stuff like everybody else. There's this store where we live that sells paintballing equipment and a couple of days later we went down there to check it out. To get into it, I mean, to get the right stuff that they sell in there, it's like three hundred dollars. So, I had about a hundred that I saved from Christmas, and I knew I'd be getting some more money from my birthday, so we all started figuring out how we were going to get the stuff. I started doing some chores around the house to make some money, and we were all just trying to get the money together. We went and rented stuff again, and it was kind of lame again, but we thought that if we got the good gear, it would be a lot more fun.

So, anyway, it took a couple of months to get all the money together, and we were still sort of into it, but it had become like this thing to get the stuff, and like that was more important anymore than really going out and doing it. The money kind of stopped meaning anything. It was like, just kind of how close you were to getting your stuff. So, I finally got all my paintball stuff, and a couple of my friends did too, but some of the guys didn't.

We got our stuff and then had to ask our parents for the money to go. I mean, you know, to get in and buy air (you need compressed air to make the guns work) and for paintballs and stuff. We didn't really figure on needing this, but we did. So we go with all our new stuff, and get out there, and it's really cool to have a fast gun and everything, but we still kind of get slammed, and it's really not much different than when we used the crappy stuff. We went a couple of more times, but then it was summer, and it was getting too hot with all that gear on, so we kind of got over it.

So now, summer's over, and I've started high school, and am trying out for the soccer team, and nobody is very interested in paintballing anymore. It was such a big deal, and we were all running around trying to get the money, and we only went a couple of times, and now all that stuff is just in the bottom of my closet, and I can't even sell it, because nobody's into it anymore. Now, there's a bunch of other stuff I wish I had, and I wish I had that three hundred dollars instead of all the paintball crap. If it had only taken longer to save the money, we would have probably been over it before we bought everything, and had the money now. I guess, sometimes you save for something, and by the time you're done saving, you don't really want it that bad anymore.

Nick—15

DEATH AND TAXES

To see how your budget should work, and what you need to think about, let's look at a part of a plan for purchasing a $3,000 car. If you are earning $6 per hour, the car is then worth five hundred of your hours ($3,000 divided by $6), right? Wrong! It is worth more than five hundred of your hours, because if you work at almost any job in this country, you will have *taxes* withheld from your paycheck. This is something you can *absolutely* expect about life! Benjamin Franklin once said, "nothing can be said to be certain except death and taxes." This is what he was talking about. For the most part, these "withholding taxes" are going to be the most expensive things in your life. Unless you are quite unusual, you will end up spending more money on taxes than you will on any other single thing. This is the first thing you should adjust your budget and your thinking for.

You can figure that the amount of the income tax withholding will be around 40 percent of what you earn. That's a lot! Forty cents out of every dollar you earn will probably be withheld from your paycheck. Know this, expect this, and plan for this. It's not a bad idea to learn how to do your own tax return when the time comes so that you can really see how taxes work. You will be doing a lot of tax returns in your life, probably about fifty or sixty of them.

Back to the example, you think you are earning $6 per hour because that's what they told you. Instead, you should be thinking that you are earning only $3.60 per hour ($6 minus 40 percent for taxes [6 times 0.6]). Now the $3,000 car is worth 833 of your hours ($3,000 divided by $3.60), right? Wrong again! We're still not done with taxes! You also have to pay sales tax on most things you can buy. Sales tax can be another 7 to 10 percent, so the $3,000 car will actually cost you $3,210 (at 7 percent sales tax [3,000 times 1.07]). In some states, they call this registration. The Life Lesson here is that whether you are in high school or you are an international investment banker, whenever you think about money, you have to think in terms of *taxes*. Don't think about what you make—*think about what you end up with* (the business term for this is "net"). Even if you go to another country, they will have taxes too! Remember Uncle Ben: death, and taxes!

❋ ❋ ❋

DARTH CREDIT

We've got to take a minute to talk about credit. Credit allows you to buy something now without having to save for it. Credit is a great thing if you have an emergency. Credit is a horrible thing when used for regular old stuff. If you only remember one thing from this whole section, let that thing be: "*If you can't pay cash for something, you really can't afford it!*" Credit card companies charge up to 20 percent interest for this service. *Avoid credit like the plague!* Remember that without interest, it takes the same amount of time to pay something off as it does to save for it. But with credit, there *is* interest, and it is a lot. Using credit to buy things makes everything at least 20 percent more expensive. It's stupid to pay 20 percent more than everybody else just because you are in a hurry!

* * *

Now to complete this example. If you want to buy the $3,000 car, you will need to work for 891 hours ($3,210 divided by $3.60) to get it. If you look at this from a different angle, the $3,000 car cost you 891 hours of work. You can now see that the amount you are really "earning" per hour is only $3.37 ($3,000 divided by 891 hours). The $6 you supposedly "earn" only buys $3.37 worth of stuff. This is why I said earlier that when you think about spending money, think that you have to earn almost two dollars for every dollar you spend! If you bought the car on credit at 15 percent interest, the car would cost an extra $481 ($3,210 times 0.15), and this reduces your $6 wage down to only $2.92 in "purchasing power." ($3,691 divided by $3.60 is 1,025 hours; as before $3000 divided by 1,025 hours equals your earning power.) Buying a car on credit is not as wise a choice as to save your money to purchase the car directly.

So how long will that take? If you work eight hours per day, five days a week (forty hours a week), this means that it will take you twenty-two weeks, almost six months to get the car (891 divided by 40), right? Wrong yet again! To do this, you have to first live through these twenty-two weeks, and living costs money too! Say as a high school student, your "living expenses" are $35 per week (lunch, gas, entertainment, etc.). This means that your living expenses chew up almost ten hours of each week's work

($35 divided by $3.60). You are really only working about thirty-one hours per week toward your "spendable" or "savable" income (nine hours going to cover your living expenses). So a realistic plan for getting this car will involved saving $110 per week (40 hours x $6 per hour less 40 percent for taxes [x 0.6] less $35 per week for living expenses). You will have to follow this plan for twenty-nine weeks instead of just twenty-two ($3,210 divided by $110) to get the car. It is realistic to plan that it will take you about seven months to save for this car—and only if you stick with this plan. This is how your budget should be figured out.

The car is worth seven months of your "frozen energy." You may say, "But that's a long time, I want it now!" Tough—this is the first aspect of how time and money are entwined. You have to remember that the seven months is going to happen to you whether you want it to or not. Either you can have some sort of plan and end up with a car, or have no plan and end up with nothing!

OPPORTUNITY HAS A PRICE TAG

Let's take it a step further. Say your $6 per hour comes from making French fries at McDonald's. Let's say that you find out that you can get a job as a lifeguard at the beach and earn $12 per hour. In order to be a lifeguard, though, you have to pass a month-long training program. At $12 per hour you will be able to get the car in only three months (40 hours x $12 per hour—40 percent [x 0.6]—0.07 percent [x 0.93] less $35 per week). Notice that this is *less* than half the time, even though your income doubled. Shouldn't it be equal, twice the money, half the time? No! Your "living" expenses are now a smaller percentage of your total wages. Because your "fixed" living expense becomes a smaller portion of your take home pay, you can save a larger portion and get the car in *less* than half the time. Money is a tricky thing!

So in order to "afford" the chance to make more money ($12 per hour instead of $6), you first have to save enough to meet your living expenses during your training period, the month in which you will be earning nothing. You need gas in your gas tank. This is a trap that catches many, many people because in the real, adult world, most people's living expenses are equal to, or even more than, their income. It's far different when your living expenses are 100 percent of your income (paying for housing, insurance, kids, and so on) instead of only 10 percent like they are for you right now. Most adults are so busy trying to get enough gas to get around that they never have enough to get ahead. This is what is meant when people say, "It takes money to make money." Don't let this happen to you. It makes for a very miserable way to live. Start stashing some dough away. NOW!

There is another very important concept hidden here. This is the concept of "lost opportunity." Your time (those pesky seven or eight inches) is all you will ever have to deal with. Every hour that goes by is gone forever and you can never get it back. If you had the chance to make $6 in that hour and you chose not to, it is the same thing as if you spent or lost that $6. If you had a chance to make $12 for that hour and you only made $6, you still lost $6. During that month you spent training for the life-guard job, you lost the income you would have received by working at McDonald's. You have to think about it as "paying" $576 (40 hours per week for 4 weeks at $6 per hour, less 40 percent) for the *right* to earn the $12 per hour. This is another big lesson about money. There is always a "cost" involved in bettering your circumstances, and this is a great thing to save up for—it is always better than saving for a material thing. You can only make the $12 per hour if you can afford to not make the $576.

You might not get this right away because you have "pretend" living expenses, and you don't need much money to get by week to week. This is because your parents pay for your "real" living expenses. Their living expenses are very important to them. If they can't pay them, you all end up living in a cardboard box! This is why savings is so important when you are working to "afford" the chance to improve your circumstances. It is quite expensive for a family to just live for a month; to have enough cash to get by without a month's income might be an expensive proposition. If your income is not so great to start with, it may take quite a while to save this much, but saving for this may still be a much better move than saving for a new television! Like with the $3,000 car example, this $576 "investment" in bettering your circumstances got you the car three months earlier, and the fact that you will continue to be making $12 and hour is just an added bonus! This is how money works.

THIS PLACE LOOKS EXPENSIVE!

To get a better feel for the real living expenses your parents face each month (sometimes referred to as their "nut"), I've itemized some of the things you have probably never thought much about. It's important for you to see these things so that you might appreciate what goes into keeping a roof over your head, as well as getting an understanding of the various expenses you are going to eventually face yourself. Expenses are yet another thing you will be able to count on in life.

Housing:	**Transportation:**
rent or mortgage	auto payments/leases
property tax	registration
property insurance	auto insurance
maintenance	gas
association dues	maintenance
repairs/deposits	repairs

Utilities:	**Health:**
gas	medical insurance
electricity	dental insurance
water	doctor's "co-pay"
sewer	prescriptions
garbage	dentistry
phone (home/cell)	optical
cable/Internet	pregnancy/illness

This is all stuff that has to be paid for each and every month just to maintain a certain lifestyle and keep a roof over your head. One way or another, everyone is paying for all these things every month. These are the "just so you can function" costs, and they don't include such "big ticket" items like food, entertainment, clothing, furniture, credit cards, fees, travel, and *emergencies!* Yes, there will always be emergencies, things you didn't plan for. It's not really that you didn't plan for them, just that your plan wasn't complete. Believe it or not, you can anticipate most things that are seen as "emergencies" when they happen. You should add them to your plan!

For example, if you have a car, you can count on the fact that something on your car will break or need to be repaired—always, every time. This will be around $1,000 a year depending on the condition of your car. If you put away $100 a month (budget for it), even though your car's running just fine, when it does break, you'll have enough to fix it right away. If you haven't done this, the emergency strikes, you don't have the money, and you don't have the car. If you can't somehow borrow the money, you might not be able to get to work, and if you can't get to work, you will probably get fired. You end up with no money, no car, and no job. Things can go downhill very quickly when it comes to money, and the sooner you learn to plan, especially to plan for the "unexpected," the sooner you will start to earn your freedom from money and be on the road to becoming rich! You can "plan" on getting sick, on getting hurt, on getting parking tickets— lots of stuff.

When thinking about these "nut" issues, the money you "must" spend every month—you will need to know that this number, whatever it is—gets bigger and bigger as time goes by. As you get older, you get more stuff and have more responsibility, and this costs more money. I mention this because of the issue of bettering your circumstances; taking time away from working to get a better skill or profession will cost more and more, year after year, as you mature. When your monthly "nut" is $1,000, you only need to save $1,000 to be able to afford the month it might take to get a better job. When your monthly "nut" is $5,000, you need to save $5,000 to afford that month of time. You can easily end up not making enough money to be able to save for bettering your circumstances. This is the "black hole" of money! This is why you should think very hard about getting whatever education or training you want *early on*. This will put you way ahead of the game, and you will get that education or training at a bargain price!

To recap here a bit about your budget, you should be thinking about income and expense. Be as realistic about both as you can. Remember that getting paid $6 per hour doesn't put six bucks in your pocket. Think about all the expenses you have as well as the ones you are going to have. Be prepared because the "future" comes like a freight train. Think about budgeting to save some money to be able to better your circumstances, and some more money to be prepared for what other people consider "emergencies." *Write this all down and keep track of it*. If you do this stuff, I guarantee that you will always have enough money, and who on Earth would not want to be in that boat? Do the work, get the reward!

YOU'RE ONLY WORTH WHAT SOMEONE IS WILLING TO PAY

Let's go back to the Value of Energy concept and how you can get the most value for your own energy. The Value of Energy relates to what someone is able to do with it. If being "meat" is your only value, moving this from here to there (that is, performing manual labor as your profession), the value of your time or energy is pretty low. Working with the energy value of your *muscles* is typically the least amount of value you will receive for your time. Working a physical *skill* (being a carpenter, plumber, mechanic, and so on) is the next step up in the value of your energy. Working with your *brain* is generally the next step (sales, customer service, bookkeeper, assistant), and the final step is to work with a *brain skill* or with your *imagination* (doctor, lawyer, accountant, architect, designer). For these, you get the greatest value for your energy, but all roads are not open to everyone! Each step takes a certain amount of training or education and not everyone has the same talents or abilities. Not everyone is cut out to be a rocket scientist. Your plan needs to be realistic and you need a really good handle on your capabilities: "Do I really have what it takes to be an engineer? Am I willing to put in the work?"

This concept may seem like a downer, but there are a few ways to get around this value stuff if that's what you want to do. It's worthwhile to mention it for your planning process. As there are only twenty-four hours in every day, for everyone, it would seem the only way to make more money is to get paid more for every hour you work. Over time, you'll get raises and promotions, and you'll make more and more per hour or per year. As this goes on, though, it becomes harder to keep it up. Eventually, you hit a "ceiling" for whatever profession or trade you are in. Even the $5,000-per-hour neurosurgeon has a ceiling. He or she can only charge so much and work for so many hours. You can get around this ceiling if you want by looking at ways to make money off of other people's energy and time. This is often a good strategy for "getting ahead." You can do this by owning a business or managing a group of people. This is a great skill to learn. This is one of the easiest ways to make more money because you don't have to be particularly smart or skilled to do it. Here, you just have to concentrate on getting smart or skilled people to work for you!

Game of Work

Work is just like, kind of a big bust. Like, it can be kind of fun, sometimes, but once you start doing it all the time, it sucks. I mean, like the money is OK, and like, it's nice to meet new people and everything, but it can be really gross, like when you have to clean something up, and especially when your boss is a jerk. I mean, when I was in school, work was a lot more fun. I got to work with my girlfriends, and even though it was something you sort of had to do, it wasn't like you really had to do it, it was just like something to get out of the house and stuff.

So, I graduated from high school and everything, and wasn't really up for going to community college right away, so my folks said I had to get a real job, and start paying for stuff around the house, like they're all pissed or something that I didn't keep going to school. So, anyway, I quit the fast food place, and got this job as a receptionist at this warehouse place. My Dad's friend helped me get the job, but the place is just so gross and everything, and there's all these total loser guys working in the back, and they think they're all hot. There's this old bookkeeper woman who is always just telling me what to do all the time, and I have to get there at like seven in the morning every day. I mean, I get pretty good money, but the place is all stinky, and especially in the morning, and it's like still dark out and cold and everything, so I like really hate the place.

Anyway, I'm telling my mom how horrible everything is, and she's just like, "Well, get used to it honey, you've only got about fifty years of this left," and I'm all, "God, I hate this place!" So, my Dad's friend, the guy who owns the place or something, comes up to me one day and tells me that Constanza, that's the bookkeeper, is all pissed that I don't do enough, and he says that he knows the place stinks and everything, but that his wife is opening this tanning place with bikinis and lotions and that kind of stuff. He says that she's going to need some help, but he kind of agrees with Constanza about my attitude and everything.

So, like I really want to get out of this place, and I figure if I start doing stuff, like even though I hate it, maybe I can go work for this guy's wife and everything. This was on like a Friday. Anyway, the next week, I get all pumped, and I go in, and I really start busting my ass. On like Thursday, the guy comes up to me, and tells me that he can really see how hard I'm working, and how he wants me to talk to his wife and everything. Then he says that he really didn't have to tell me anything, like he could have just kept quiet and saw how I did, but he figured I'd really like the job at his wife's new place and everything.

So, I'm driving home, and I'm thinking that even that crappy warehouse was better when I was busting my ass. I mean, when I was busy doing stuff, the time went by a lot faster, and Constanza wasn't such a bitch all the time, and what if the guy hadn't said anything, and I was just a slacker and everything.

Anyway, I got the job with Carol, that's his wife, and it's like such a cool place, and the money's the same, and she's like really nice and everything. So, I'm working there now, and I'm still busting my ass, because I want to do good for Carol, and, like it still makes the time go by faster, and if I do good, then maybe something else is going to come up for me. Anyway, work sucks, but it can like really suck, or just sort of suck, I mean, it's kind of up to you.

Alicia—19

There is another "trick" for getting the most out of the value of your energy. To do this, you should look at all the various professions you might be interested in (and are capable of doing!). Each profession, each job that's out there, has a percentage attached to it. This is the percentage of people in that profession who make a whole bunch of money. Almost all doctors make a decent wage, and there is a very large percentage who make a lot of money. When choosing a profession such as being a sculptor, you will have to be one of the very, very best to make a comfortable living, or you could be just another starving artist. When looking at what it is you want to do for a living, you should think about these percentages. Your best bet—your "percentage shot," if you will—is always to try to find something where the "average" is high. Having to be the best at something is really hard and it means that the majority are, de facto, not the best. Keep this in mind, but still be true to yourself. *You can't ignore your own happiness when looking at money and how to make it.*

MAKE MINE A DOUBLE

Doing something you detest, with only money as the reward, is a losing strategy. Eventually, the fact that you are so unhappy doing it (regardless of whether you're good at it or not), will cause you to end up failing. Finding something that you love to do will ultimately make you the most money and bring you the most happiness because we are usually very good at things we are passionate about. You may not end up with a hundred-foot yacht or a beach house in the Caymans, but you will be much more content with your time on this planet. Think about the guy who works ten hours a day in a job he hates so that he can make enough money to go on vacation to the beach for two weeks out of every year. Wouldn't he be much happier to make less money and figure out how to live at the beach fifty-two weeks a year?

Always remember that the importance of money lies in *how you use what you have* and not in the sheer *volume*. Measuring the volume (how much money someone has, "how big their boat is") is a bad way to look at the world. Looking at money as a tool that can get you what you want is a good way to look at the world. This subtle difference in perspective makes a big difference in how much you end up with and how happy you'll be with your seven or eight inches. Learn to control your money and not let it control you. You do this with a budget.

The statement that money can't buy love or happiness is certainly true. So while money shouldn't ever become the goal in itself, never underestimate its power. While it can't buy you love or happiness, the lack of money (or lacking the ability to plan and budget what you have) will buy you a much more difficult time in life. Money is the grease that makes the machine of life run a whole lot more smoothly.

The comedian Redd Foxx was in the old TV show *Sanford and Son*. Fred Sandford's son Lamont tells him, "Money doesn't buy you happiness, Dad!" Fred replies, "Yeah, that's just what all the poor folks say so they can sleep at night!" People with money usually have little interest in other people's fortunes, while people without money are often paralyzed by how much everyone else has.

THE EARLY BIRD GETS THE WORM
(OR WHATEVER ELSE THEY WANT!)

The last part of this section about money is about the timing of money. Someone once said that "compound interest" is the seventh wonder of the world. Why this is true is because of the way the math works. If your parents invested $10,000 for you when you were born, (half the price of a new car) and it earned 10 percent interest, you would have about $74,000 by the time you were twenty, and almost $550,000 by the time you were forty. You'd have a little over $4 million by the time you were sixty, and a whopping $30 million by the time you were eighty! This is huge! This is because of the way compound interest works. It works this way because you start earning interest *on the interest.* It's like making money off of other people's energy, but here, *you* don't have to do anything but wait! I bring this up because it shows how important it is to start as early as you can. The sooner you start to pay attention to money and how it works, the sooner you will start to get ahead. It's like a foot race. It is always easier to run ahead of the pack than to run behind it. As the dogsled racers say, "If you're not the lead-dog, the view never changes." If you get ahead with your money early in your life (right now), you will find that you keep getting farther ahead as time goes on. If at some point you realize that you indeed have too much money, you can always just give it away. If, on the other hand, you find out you don't have enough, you can seldom do anything about it!

Lastly, there is a counterintuitive part to this thought. It has to do with "positioning" yourself—making sure you are at the right place at the right time. This has to do with looking way down the road in your plan. Let's go back to the $6 per hour fry cook and the $12 per hour lifeguard. Let's say this situation is not just about making money while you are in school, but that these are your only two choices in life. The lifeguard makes more right now, but that job is sort of a dead end. Maybe you could end up managing the other lifeguards, and maybe get up to $25 an hour, but that's probably it. Bearing down and sucking it up as a fry cook might be much less of a dead end. You could end up managing the restaurant ($20 per hour), managing several restaurants ($50 per hour), or even starting your own (??? per hour).

You need to keep in mind that each step you take opens some doors and closes others. Sometimes it makes sense to make more right now, sometimes it makes sense to take a little less right now if you will have more opportunity down the road. You need to think that while there is a $6 difference between the fry cook and lifeguard job now, there's a $25 difference between the lifeguard manager and the manager of a restaurant chain down the road. Sometimes you need to suck up the $6 difference to make the $25 difference.

To take this thought a step further, say that what you really want to do is own a restaurant. Very few people who work in restaurants ever end up owning one (unless they work in one owned by their father!). Sometimes you need to think about all the different paths that lead to the same place. It might be a lot easier for a commercial realtor to end up owning a restaurant than it is for the waitress (being in the position to find restaurants that are for sale), and perhaps an investment banker would have a better chance than the cook (the position to finance the purchase of a restaurant). Pay attention, be clever, be smart, try to think of all the angles, and spend a lot of time working on your plan—review it, revise it, and keep it fresh! *Write it all down*!

* * *

Key Points

This section just scratches the surface of money but should get you off to a good start. Money is relative—its value relates to your needs. Plan for what you think you'll need and think in terms of the time it takes to earn, the time it takes to save, and the timing of when you earn what you can. And budget! Start managing your money now so you can have what you want when you'll want it. Get your initial savings going and realize that you have earn almost $2 for every $1 you save or spend. Think about the "energy value" of your money and the ways you can increase it through education, training, and just plain old hard work. Never forget about taxes. Understand how $6 per hour turns into $3.60, then $3.37, then $2.85 if you're not careful.

Try to get a handle on living expenses, the "pretend" ones you have now and the real ones you'll be facing down the road. Remember that it takes money to make money, that there are ever increasing costs involved in bettering your circumstances. Plan for the emergencies you know you are going to have. Try to figure out how to make money off of other people's time and energy, but never forget to do what you really want to do. Money is just grease and not the machine itself. Write your budget and your plan down! Check it often and make it better!

❊ ❊ ❊

You should now spend a little time talking about this:

- What do you think about managing and budgeting the little bit of money you have?
- What do you think about getting some savings together to start the process?
- Do you understand how taxes, credit, and time affect your earnings?
- What do you think the "energy value" of your own time is worth?
- Do you understand the discussion about the costs of bettering your circumstances?
- What do you think about "real" living expenses? (Have your parents tell you the amounts they pay for some of this stuff and add it up. What's their "nut"?)
- Do you really get why you should be smart about money early on?

birds of a feather flock together!

(How to Be Whomever You Want to Be)

The whole Birds of a Feather concept and all their flocking habits is a biblical Fact of Life. It's about how similar people hang out together. It's pretty simple and pretty obvious, but we need to take a closer look at how we define "similar" people. Think about how quickly you can "define" a total stranger by the way he or she dresses, talks, appears, and acts. You can tell their age, perhaps where they're from, their social class (wealth), their education, perhaps even what they do for a living. This defining is somewhat new to you. As a teenager, you have probably only started to look at people this way (up to this point, adults were kind of invisible). This definition process is a big part of what teenagers learn in high school. They practice by defining one another. Learning how to define people by their social attributes (posture, clothes, attitude, speech, physical size) is an important skill to learn. These attributes all add up to what we think about that person before we have even heard a word they have to say. Our skill in doing this is a critical survival tactic for any social animal such as a human being. It helps you navigate through a world populated mostly by strangers. These skills help you identify people you might want to be friends with or those you wish to avoid.

I GOT YOUR NUMBER

To organize all these opinions we naturally have, we establish groupings of people in our heads and label these groups in many different ways. We may create some "flocks" or "groups" from our personal experiences (soccer moms, mostly harmless; gang members, great danger), and others from stories we've heard, myths in circulation (urban legends), and general prejudice (bad cops, the Russian Mafia, Jews, gays and lesbians). This is called "stereotyping," fitting all kinds of individuals into neat little groups that we then believe certain "generalities" about (whether they are true or not). While we've always been told it is a bad thing to do, I am here to disagree. Stereotyping is not bad or good in itself—it's just part of the way our brains work. I point this out simply so that you can understand it. Being able to recognize it when done by yourself or others is quite helpful. This section is all about stereotypes and "flocks/groups," and how they are defined, what they do for us, and how we can use them (and the understanding of them) to be whomever we wish to be.

When we see a particular individual, we instantly try to define them by the group we think they belong to, and attach the generalities we believe about the group to the individual. We are all people-watchers and we all stereotype. ("That pretty girl over there wearing the nice clothes thinks she's all that, and is probably so into herself that talking to her would just be a waste of time," or "That nerdy little guy over there is probably some brainiac geek.") If you think about it, you probably spend a lot of time identifying people this way. It's OK—it's what people do.

Identifying a dangerous character on the street can keep you from harm. In fact, immediate identification is so important that people we may need are given uniforms to make them more recognizable, easier to "stereotype" (such as police, firefighters, and paramedics). We even provide them with special vehicles so we can see them a long way off. We give them sirens and flashing lights. We make it very easy to identify them. But we also identify businesspeople, teachers, housewives, and virtually any person we see wandering around. We think in terms of these group identities and even adjust our actions to suit each one. (How differently do you act in front of a group of cheerleaders than you do a group of cops?)

CLIQUES AND CLACKS

We begin learning these skills during the teenage years, and that's why this knowledge becomes such a huge deal in high school. It's the first time in your life that you really become aware of your own existence as an individual distinct from your family. It's the first time you are part of a group ("your crew, dude") that's not your family. You find that the kids you used to just hang out with have somehow evolved into a group. At school, your group has an identity and you have an identity inside your group. Your group listens to you and cares about what you think. You are a big shot in your group. You concoct all kinds of crazy ways of looking at the world and the people outside your group just don't get it (this is the birth of the inside joke).

Without paying much attention, you and your friends suddenly become a group, and you, as a member of the group, are now identified by its characteristics, not necessarily yours! You have been stereotyped—or more accurately, you have stereotyped yourself. Whether you like it or not, the same way you look at other people in other groups is also the way everyone else is looking at you. This is the whole key to this section: While you're so busy stereotyping everyone else, you might forget that you, too, are being stereotyped by others! Really getting this thought through your head is a huge step in becoming whomever you want to be.

We'll get back to this concept in a minute, but there are a few other things you should know about groups. People (those who are outside of your group) give you and your group definition, and one of the interesting things about these definitions is that they usually "define" you by what you're *not*. Groups are more often defined by what they're not or what they're against, than for what they are or what they favor. It's always easier to drop a clear "against" sound bite ("I hate preppies"), than to define what you are for ("...skateboarding kids who are not punks, but like punk music, but not all punk music, and who are smart, but not too smart...").

Groups are going to be a very big part of your life, and this is an excellent way to begin to understand how they work. Groups create the worlds we choose to live in—from buddies at school, to fraternity brothers or sorority sisters in college, to doctors or businesspeople or golfers, it's group after group after group. Some of your groups will overlap (two friends from this group are also in that group), and some are distinct. You can draw little circles on a piece of paper to indicate all the groups you already belong to (buddies, soccer team, band, immediate family, extended family, employee, and so on).

Amateur Hour

The worst thing about being a teenager is that everyone, especially parents, does nothing but give you advice. Kids hate advice. Everyone hates being told what to do. I graduated from high school a year ago, and was so glad to be done with it. I'm now in a state college, and I work at a clothing store. Life has changed a lot. Probably the biggest thing that has changed for me, is that I'm a lot more interested in advice now, in what certain people have to say. I've learned to pay more attention to people who've kind of been there and done that.

The worst part for me, I mean the part that made me really mad about myself, was when I realized that I was trying to get advice from all these people I thought I should be listening to, people who were going through the same stuff as me. You know, my friends. It was like this big moment, because I suddenly realized that what I really needed was not to be talking to people who were going through the same stuff, but people who had gone through the same stuff, and made it through to the other side. Although it makes you feel better to talk to someone who really understands what's going on, and says yeah, yeah, yeah, this really doesn't give you any help, and the help is what you really need. I was talking to my friends, and they were all sympathetic and helped me feel sorry for myself, but it didn't get me anywhere!

I didn't want to listen to the people who were telling me about the things I had to do, the work I had to do, the stuff that wasn't fun. I was ignoring the advice I was getting from the people I would learn to really respect, and just feeling sorry for myself. It was like having a medical problem or something, and going to a plumber, someone who understood the problem but had no idea how to fix it. When you're thinking about your life, and the things you should be doing, you should be asking questions from someone who has been there and done it successfully, not a bunch of amateurs. No matter how much your friends care about you, they're amateurs at life, and when it comes to your life, you need to listen to the pros! That's the real deal. The kids you hang with don't really have a clue, but you end up depending on them to help you with really complicated problems. Your parents, or other adults who are really concerned about you, have been through really similar stuff, but you just blow them off, because you think they don't understand. They do understand. It's you who doesn't understand. You get all pissed off because they don't tell you what you want to hear. Your friends tell you what you want to hear, but they are just as clueless as you are.

Now that I'm in college and working, I find that when I really have something that's bothering me, I go to my mom or my dad. I still talk to my friends, and they have changed a lot too, but now I realize that they are just as screwed up as I am, and that their advice is not really worth that much. Most of them have more problems than I do, so why should I be looking to them to help me out?

Kelly–20

WE ARE FAMILY

In school, you've got jocks, nerds, goths, punks, preppies, gang-bangers, druggies, weirdoes—however you choose to define and label everybody. Group after group after group, and you have definitions for all of them, just like they have for you! You spend more time practicing these kind of social skills in high school than you spend on any particular subject being taught in the class room. Think about when you introduce someone to someone else. The first thing you do is define their group, how they came to be with you ("This is Susan, my friend," or "I know Ralph from soccer," or "Tom and I work together."). Groups are a really, really big thing in life.

The high school years are a period in life when we first start to participate in this whole group identification thing, and as these new groups grow in importance to us, our previous groups diminish in importance. This is the period where you begin to distance yourself from your family and define yourself by whatever group you have fallen into. This is a big part of getting ready for the next stage of your life—that is, being on your own, inch three. It's a very subtle thing. Without even paying much attention, you have become a group, a clique of like-minded buddies. This bonding is very powerful and necessary to our own identity (even those without a group are given a group—the loners). The problem is that we don't really choose our group—they just sort of happen.

Your group is all about conforming to the attributes of the buddies you choose to hang with. You talk alike, dress alike, act alike, and listen to the same music and watch the same movies and TV shows—you spend a hell of a lot of time making it easy for other people to label you and know what group you are in. This is funny to me because any high school student will go to great lengths to tell you how unique and individual and independent they are. Look around! You wouldn't be caught dead wearing the wrong clothes, make up, or cap—or whatever it is that defines the group you've accidentally become a part of. You draw great distinction between being a goth or a punk. You are spending most of your adolescent time conforming to the rules of your group and the development of distinctions between other groups ("Like, oh my god, *they* are just like so totally weird!"). Don't be defensive. Don't say it isn't true. Don't think you're so unique. You are trying really hard not to be unique! This has been going on since the first high school opened its doors. Groups, group dynamics, social interaction, defining, and labeling is everything to a high school student. Understand it for what it is and use it to get what you want.

You're known by the company you keep— birds of a feather flock together, after all. This is important to think about because it stays with you for your whole life; it's the way we structure a very complicated world so that we can have an easier time dealing with it. To begin using this knowledge, imagine that you are not only known by the company you keep, but also by the company you don't keep! You can control what group you're in, and thereby control what people think about you. It isn't easy, because the whole point of all these groups is to organize a complicated world. When someone moves from one group to another, it upsets the balance and forces people to "reorganize" their world too. You can't just start sitting at the lunch table with the "cool" kids—it's weird. As an experiment, if you're so inclined, go to school one day wearing completely different clothes than you usually do and see the commotion it creates.

CORRECT CHANGE REQUIRED
You have to change groups slowly and give everyone time to adjust. You do it by giving people a reason to adjust their

thinking about you. You do this by asserting your individuality, and this is a very mature and grown-up thing to learn how to do correctly. You do this by earning the respect of those you want to respect you. Respect is never given, it's never just deserved, it's always earned! As we learned about money, earning takes time; you need a plan into the future. You have to do this by seeing yourself as others see you, and not as you see yourself. You see yourself as a "cool" guy or girl in your group. An adult sees you as just another punk teenager. How do you think these definitions differ? I hope you would say, "Quite a bit!"

Then why is it so hard to understand that by acting differently, you can greatly influence what others think about you and what group they put you in? If you give them a reason, they will change their opinion—without a reason, they probably won't change. How much do you change your behavior on a job interview or a date to give someone a reason to have respect for you? Why don't you do this *all* the time? This is how you become whomever you want to be. Just like with everything else in this book, it just takes some thinking, a plan, and the effort to put the plan forward.

You're probably saying this is all well and good, but you *like* your group, you don't want to change. You feel nice and safe and secure in your warm and fuzzy group. Understandably, you don't want it to change. Think about your direction in life. Is your group getting you closer or farther away? Is it really *your* goal and direction that you're moving toward, or the goals and directions of your group? Although you think they are totally cool, what do others really think? Have you really made a conscious choice? If you had a clean slate, would you choose a different group? Would you choose to be defined in a different manner?

Really look at how you fit into the world. Look at this from other people's perspectives. How big of a fish are you in *their* pond? This works every time. You can be in any group you want by looking at the world from that group's perspective and fitting into their "organizational" structure (into all their stereotypes). You can be with the cool kids, you can date whom you want, you can get jobs, you can do anything by taking this "outside-in" look at yourself. At 17, you look at someone who's 47 as being pretty old, while a 70 year old looks at them as a punk. Perspective is the great equalizer.

COMMAND AND CONTROL

To get people to look at you in a different light, you must first look at yourself in this different light. You may think that you "look" just fine, but take a minute here, put the book down, and find a full-length mirror somewhere in your house. Go by yourself and physically look at yourself in the mirror. (I'm sure you do this all the time.) This time though, try to look at yourself as someone else would look at you. Think about how they would stereotype you. Look at your clothes, your hair, your posture, your general cleanliness. What do you think an adult really sees when they look at you? Think about how they would respect you.

What would you change to take control of this process and be the person you would want to be? You're being silly if you really think everything is fine, that you're perfect. Human nature is to want to change ourselves. The problem is that we are always afraid to do it because of what people might think! That's the whole damn point! You should want to change what people think about you. You should want to control how they see you.

You can change your hair, your clothes, or your look in many different ways, but this is not totally what I'm talking about. (Although it may be a part of it if you look particularly hideous). Your outside looks are the things that give people "clues" as to who you are, but changing only your appearance is just like putting the same old crappy cereal in a new box. You can fool everyone once, but to make a difference you've got to change the cereal, make it something someone would like! You have to change your insides. You have to change your attitude, what image you project to the outside world.

A MAN IN FULL

To talk about changing the "who you are" into the "who you want to be," no one has figured it out any better than an ancient Greek guy named Epictetus (*ê-pik-teè-tus*). He lived in first-century Rome (two thousand years ago). He was a slave and had a particular passion for freedom and independence (just like teenagers do). He had a pretty miserable life. He was crippled because he was so mistreated as a slave. As he got older, he eventually could not work hard enough and was thrown out on the streets to starve. (And you think you've got it rough!) Rome was not a pretty place then. Nero was emperor and people were routinely rounded up and thrown in the coliseum to be mauled by wild animals. Murder, rape, and crime were rampant. (One theory as to the great fire that engulfed the city during this period—remember Nero "fiddling" while Rome burned?—is that it was set on purpose to "cleanse" the city of how bad it had become.)

Anyway, Epictetus was thrown into this city an exslave with nothing to his name. He had a pretty crappy "boat" and was grouped in a pretty horrible "group." He began teaching philosophy in the marketplace and was so profound, his teaching so powerful, that he became one of the most influential people in the city. He was teacher to a teenager named Marcus Aurelius, who eventually became the emperor who led Rome to what is considered its Golden Age.

Epictetus taught many things and it would be quite worthwhile to find one of his books (although they are surprisingly hard to come by) to study his thinking in depth. For the purposes of this book, I will just touch on some of the high points.

Endure and Renounce.

Epictetus understood groups very well. He knew that first you had to endure the judgments of others because you cannot control them yourself. However, through self-reliance, being all you can be to yourself, you can change these judgments over time by renouncing their hold on you. This is all about putting yourself above the judgments of others. Don't ignore that people judge you, but don't let those judgments control how you act.

Responsibility for Good and Evil.

Epictetus claimed that nothing in the world is "good" or "evil" in itself, that we attach these values to everything, and different people attach different values to the same thing. How we judge determines how we'll be judged! I think Epictetus had a big impact on the early Christians who began showing up in Rome at this time. ("Let he who has not sinned cast the first stone," and "Judge not, lest ye be judged.") Epictetus claimed that every man bears the *exclusive* responsibility himself for his own good or evil, that this is our "free will," and cannot consist of any of the things others can do *to* us or *for* us. In other words, there are no excuses—you're responsible whether you like it or not! Honor is born of responsibility. Do the right thing only because it's the right thing, not for some reward or to avoid some harm.

Highest Good Lies in Reason.

Here, it's how and what we think that makes us who we really are; our ultimate happiness is determined by what we consciously allow ourselves to desire or avert (in other words, our *choices*). Failing to attain what we desire or encountering what we wish to avoid creates all people's passions and sorrows, so we should control our desires and aversions, thereby controlling our passions and happiness. Understand what you *choose* to desire or avoid. Wake up and smell the coffee. Pay attention to what you're doing.

Great Expectations

It was just one thing after another. God, I don't know what was going on! It all started when I got my car when I was 16. It was a four-wheel drive Tahoe that was totally cool, even though it was used. A couple days after I got it, I was pretty stupid. I was driving a friend around, and I knew I wasn't supposed to do that, but we were screwing around, and there was this little hill where he lived. I drove over a curb, over the sidewalk, and up the hill to where I thought there was an open field. There wasn't. There was this big drainage thing and the Tahoe got stuck. It took two tow trucks to get it out.

Anyway, I got in trouble and got grounded. I thought the grounding was unfair, and I guess I had kind of a bad attitude about the whole thing. At least that's what my folks kept going on and on about. I did some other stupid stuff, got in more trouble, got the Tahoe taken away, and was even more bummed. My grades started to suck, and my Mom just got out of control, so I went to live with my Dad. I went to summer school, and things were pretty mellow, but then when regular school started again, there was more trouble building up, and I got drunk on a friend's parent's boat, and now my Dad was out of control too, so I went back to my Mom's.

It went on like this all junior year. I'd get in trouble, would be pissed about the punishment, would get in more trouble, and go back and forth between my Mom and Dad's houses. I started hanging out with different friends, and ended up doing meth and smoking pot and drinking and stuff. My Dad kicked me out of his house, and then my Mom kicked me out of her's. I spent a couple of weeks just living out of my car, and that sucked. My folks finally got together with me, and told me I could come home, and I did, but the first weekend I spent with my Dad, I took off after he went to sleep and got caught hiding in this girl's closet by her Mom.

It was just one thing after another, and everything was so screwed up, and I just wanted to graduate, and be on my own, where everyone wasn't constantly telling me what to do. Everything sucked, and I started thinking about what I was doing, and why things were such a mess. I thought that I just kept getting in trouble for stupid stuff, and I was getting in trouble because I kept thinking that I could do stuff and not get caught, but I kept getting caught!

Then I thought, instead of expecting to always get away with stuff, what if I just expected to get caught all the time. When I started thinking this way, it made me stop being so stupid. I'd think, if I do this and get caught, I'll be in a whole lot of trouble, and like, is it really worth it? I stopped doing stupid stuff, and stopped getting in trouble. When I wasn't in trouble, I wasn't pissed off all the time, and didn't get in more trouble. I guess I kind of grew up when I figured this all out.

Ben—19

Epictetus's message is very similar to the inspired thinking behind the Serenity Prayer: "Grant me the serenity to accept the things I cannot change, the courage to change the things I can, and the wisdom to know the difference."

This should be your big take-away regarding Epictetus. What he says is that much of what goes on in the world, the vast majority of things that happen, and are happening, are completely, 100 percent out of your control. You cannot control much, and that desire to control what you can't leads to misery. He says that, in fact, you can only control three things—how you act, what you think, and how you let things affect you. This is all about the "groups" and "flocks" we talked about earlier, and perceptions and forms of identification associated with them.

You can choose to act however you wish, and you are doing this minute by minute, every day. This should be the result of your free will and constant attention, and not just willy-nilly, go-with-the-flow kind of stuff—not just acting like other people "expect" you to act.

You can control what you think and how you think, and this, too, is how you exercise your free will and *actively* influence the world around you.

Most importantly, and not so immediately obvious, is that you can control how you let things affect you. If someone calls you a "weenie" in the hallway, do you fly into a rage, do you dwell on what that person thinks? Should you even care? Should you think that you have a problem, or that they have the problem? You have a choice in the matter, and you give people power over you by bowing to their perceptions, by "letting" those people affect you!

You are the only one who knows your own truth, and this should be all that matters to you. Be honorable and you will be honored. Be deserving of respect and you will be respected. It comes from inside yourself, and over time, all but the most stupid will see you for who you have become. This is the only way you can break the power of groups and people stereotyping you into a neat, little box. Exercise your free will to be true to yourself and you can be whomever you want to be.

❈ ❈ ❈

Key Points

I hope you can see that we are constantly defining people by their social attributes, we are constantly stereotyping, and that other people are just as busy doing the same thing to us! Think about the groups you belong to and how you came to belong to them. Think about what your peers believe and what they are against. Think about the direction of your group. Is it your direction? Think about how new groups have emerged for you and how your old groups have faded away. Do you know the reasons? Understand how groups work and how you can actively choose the people with whom you wish to be associated. Really assert your individuality, thinking about your direction in life and whether your groups are getting you closer or farther away. Learn to look at yourself as others see you. You can control your outside appearance and you can control your inside composition, who you really are. Remember Epictetus! Seek out what you desire and avoid what you detest. Know that a lot of what goes on in the world is outside your ability to control and concentrate instead on how you act, how you think, and most importantly, how you let things affect you.

* * *

You should now spend a little time talking about this:

- What do you think about stereotypes?
- How did you come to be a part of your group?
- How do you think adults would define you?
- How can you assert your individuality?
- What would you change about your outside appearance or your inside?
- What do you think about Epictetus, the idea of what you can control and what you can't?
- How can you control the way you let things affect you?

Section Eight

blood is thicker than water!

(How You Should "Use" Your Family)

Blood being "thicker" than water is biblical reference. Most people understand it as meaning that the bond to your "family group" is an obligation—that "blood" should come first in your dealings with the world (all your other groups who are not part of your family). It is understood as an admonishment, telling you that you must think this way or you'll be in big trouble. It's seen as a demand that the priorities of your family group be set high above your other groups and relationships (the ones that are so much more fun), and that you must be more responsible to your family. You get the sense from this that you *owe* your family, and this debt makes you rebellious because you don't like the "work" a family requires. You would rather just have fun.

This "work" makes you want to complain to your friends that your family is such a drag. (I have to do this and that, and I have to go here and there, and I have to say this or that.) This makes you not want to take out the trash. Nevertheless, you have to really think about family and what it means to understand why taking out the trash is a good thing (and not just because it smells). You need to think about taking out the trash because of the counterintuitive side of blood being thicker than water.

WHAT IF THE HOKEY-POKEY *IS* WHAT IT'S ALL ABOUT?

If you look at it from outside in, it's not about your obligation to your family, but your family's obligation to *you* that you should be paying attention to. When I say "family," I don't just mean your mother or father, I mean the whole ball of wax— aunts, uncles, grandparents, brothers, sisters, cousins, nieces, and nephews. You'll never know when someone can be of great assistance to you! Blood being thicker than water should simply let you know that as you face the great big world out there, your family group will be the longest lasting, most genuinely supportive group you will ever be a part of.

The Life Lesson here is: When you need your family to be there for you, you're going to be damn glad you were there for them. It's not only about what you can do for your family, but what they can do for you (to butcher the old JFK quote)! This is why blood being thicker than water is important. It's a Fact of Life. You can count on the fact that many times in the future, you are going to need the support only your family can (and is willing to) give. It's kind of like a bank account. You can count on the fact that you will be needing to make a withdrawal in the future, so you better put some deposits in while you can.

Blood being thicker than water implies that we should be especially good to our family "because" we will want them to be especially good to us. This is all about the future, knowing that you will face a crisis (perhaps many) down the road. When the chips are down, your family will be the only ones you can really count on. This is the big Fact of Life! It's a good idea to test this theory and prove to yourself that it's true. Go to your friends and tell them that you have a really big problem, that you need $200 right away. Be serious—tell them that you can't really get into why you need the money, but that you need it in twenty-four hours. See if they come up with the money. See if they really come through. Don't imagine this test, do it! See who actually hands you the cash.

My Homeys

Yeah, I got my group, my homeys. We're tight, and not just like a bunch of posers. So, it was like a couple of weeks ago, I'm just chilling, and it's like Saturday and everything and it's like Shawn with the big 911. Him and some of the other dudes are all at the mall and everything, just hanging, and there's like a bunch of these straight edger kids, and they're all like trying to oust them and everything, and there's like thirty of them or something, and just like three of us—not like me, but our dudes.

So, we're all calling and everything, and we're all set to "kick it" at this park around eight. It's this city versus city thing. We're calling, and getting everybody together and getting rides and everything, and it's all pipes and chains and shit. So, we're all just totally into it and going to kick some ass. I mean straight edgers are all into doing nothing, and just like fighting, and we're all, "that's so messed up," and everything. I mean, straight edgers are supposed to be all against drugs and sex and everything, but they fight all the time, and can't just chill. They're trying to bust us and everything, so we're going to get into it at eight.

Anyway, we get there, I mean, my ride and me and another dude, and there's all these cars and everything, and we're all like, "Whoa, dude." We get out, and it's all kind of messed up where we had to park and everything, and we're walking over, and we're seeing all these dudes. There's like a whole bunch of them and everything, and we're walking over to our side, and we hear this car screaming down the road and everything, and we're all like, just standing there. So anyway, the car like just screeches to a stop, like right where we're standing, and the lights go on and everything, and the doors fly open, and we're just, like right in the headlights—just standing there. We're like, so busted! It's the cops!

So, I turn to see what's going on, and I see everybody just running and everything, and the cops got their guns out, and are telling us not to move. I'm looking behind me, and I see

Johnny and the other dudes, the first dudes that were at the Mall, Johnny was the dude that called me, and he's all running and everything, but he sees me, and we just look at each other. So, Johnny, and everybody else all got away, and we got busted, and we didn't "kick it" or anything. I mean, I had this knife and everything, and now my folks have to take me to court, but I was there dude, I was all tight with my homeys.

Vince–17

Family lasts a lot longer than friends, but you haven't been alive long enough to see how this works. There is a "currency" to family obligations (both to and from you), and this currency is good will. It's about feeling good about them and them feeling good about you. Families, whether they are aware of it or not, expect problems (some revel in them), but it's a two-way street, and if your family bank account (your good will) runs too dry, they will begin to cut their losses. You'll find them being there less and less. I can promise you that eventually you are going to need a loan from this family currency (perhaps many), and you're going to need it big time. Sock some deposits away now!

PASS THE PEAS, PLEASE

As the saying goes, "They may not be much, but they're all you got!" You should think about your family in this light. Teenagers, thinking they're immortal and the centers of their own universe, seldom realize the longevity of family. Teenagers are so caught up in the here-and-now that they don't think forward to that Christmas dinner when they'll be 35 years old. You will be at this dinner. Your family will be at this dinner. You will all be eighteen years older and a lot of stuff will have happened in those eighteen years. (Remember, the future is a freight train, and you're not going to stop it.) You'll be sitting there with your family and you will probably be very thankful for the many times during those eighteen years that they bailed you out—financially, emotionally, or physically!

Hopefully, they will also be thankful for the many times you were there for them. If you remember reading this book, you will think about all the friends over those eighteen years that were as helpful, and my guess is that there won't be many. A family has "legs," or staying power, while friends can sometimes come and go like the weather. This is a Fact of Life—you just haven't been around long enough to see it in action.

Families are accidents, "groups" that just happen, and all families are not like what we see on television or what we would like to imagine. Families are like solar systems. For the most part, kids orbit around their parents' "sphere of influence." Likewise, your parents may still be orbiting around their parents' sphere of influence. Traditionally, kids are locked in tight because the parents provide all the "goodies" of living, such as food, shelter, and physical and emotional comfort. The kids stay in tight until they finally strike out on their own and leave the house. They still orbit their parents—it's just that the orbit is not so tight anymore.

When these kids start families of their own, they become the center of their children's orbits, and the bond with the grandparents gets just a little weaker. Eventually, as the grandparents get older and less capable, they may end up being sucked into an orbit around their own children. At any given moment, every family has a gravitational center, a point from which all the members orbit. A family's gravitational center is ever changing.

Picture a strong, successful grandfather, a caring grandmother, and their big house with all the relatives, children (and their children) arriving for Christmas dinner. They all arrive at the gravitational center of the family. The center of a family is usually where the holiday parties are held, and that center changes over time. Part of understanding families is seeing how these spheres of influence appear, change, and adjust. You are part of it and you may end up at the center yourself someday.

If you think of a family tree, the gravitational center is the strongest branch supporting you. Each new family that sprouts from this branch can peter out as only a splinter from the main stock, or it may become the new strongest branch supporting all the future sprouts. Your family is connected by all these branches back to the very first family that could call themselves human. Some branches die out. Yours, because of the simple fact that you're alive, has not. Keeping it going is the result of thousands of years of struggle. Although families today can seem kind of isolated, don't forget that they're still all connected to the tree and all still thriving. You're the next sprout.

This picture of the traditional family is not always the case. Sometimes, with divorce, personal or financial problems, or addictions, kids have to be the gravitational center early on and the parents orbit them. This is a very tough situation, and we are all familiar with the story of the teenager keeping the family together while mom or dad or both have somehow checked out. Even in this situation, the family is still very important, perhaps more so, and still connected to the tree. Here, it's easier for the teenager to see the importance of sticking together even though the parents don't. Good Will continues to need banking. It's just that in these situations, the parents are doing most of the withdrawing while the kids are keeping up the deposits.

"HEY DAD, YOU'RE NOT GOING TO BELIEVE THIS, BUT…"

The problem with families is that when you need them, there is no substitute, but for long stretches of time they just get in your way. They want stuff from you, especially when you're a teenager. Think of this as the depositing part to the bank account. It's kind of like how someone once described war: "Long stretches of interminable boredom interrupted by tiny instances of terror, panic, and fear." While there are a lot of things about family that are extremely annoying and even upsetting, we have to put up with this troublesome stuff to get the help we are going to need when we are going to need it.

Horrible things are going to happen to you. They happen to

everyone. You can get really sick, you can get really hurt in an accident, you can be arrested, get pregnant or get someone else pregnant, lose all your money, your job, your house. You can have drug or alcohol problems. This stuff happens to a lot of people, and you should make sure you have a healthy bank account with your family so you'll be prepared when it happens to you. Your family's "being there" is not just about money. Sometimes when bad stuff happens, the thing most needed is simply the comfort of knowing that you're not alone, that someone is on your side. The Life Lesson here is that you're going to need stuff, and just like with a bank account, you can only get out of it what you've put into it!

AN OFFER YOU CAN'T REFUSE

Before we go on, we need to think a little bit about the expectations we have about our family. A family is a complicated group with a lot of ever-changing rules. It's complicated and confusing because it is the first group that everyone belongs to, and it's the only group you'll be a part of where there is never any choice involved. They don't choose you, and you don't choose them, it just happens. You're born, bam, you're part of whatever family you're in, and that's that. Likewise, it's a group you can never leave (just like the Mafia—no wonder they call it "the family"). Family is thrust upon you and you are thrust upon it, come hell or high water. The issue is that we have this picture in our heads of what a family should be and we look around ourselves and go, "Wait a minute, this can't be right!"

It's this difference between what we think a family *should* be and what it really *is* that keeps us from using our families effectively and understanding their value. To do this, we need to separate the reality from our expectations.

Today, the media, mostly television, provides almost all of our expectations about how a family or life in general should be. This is a big problem. Not long ago, expectations about family and life came from real experience and not what people saw in the media. There wasn't any media! People based their expectations about family on other real families (their grandparents, aunts, uncles, cousins, and neighbors). They based real life on real life, and this worked out pretty well because people were living in small towns and neighborhoods. Today, we don't always live in those same small towns or neighborhoods, and even if we did, we might not have very many relatives around. We barely know our neighbors. We move every couple of years—one house to the next to the next. This is where we start to get screwed up.

We don't get a chance to really know our neighbors, and typically only see our relatives on the holidays, so we have to look elsewhere for our role models, and unfortunately we look to television. We learn to expect things to be like we see them on TV. Today, we watch a lot of TV, and the characters in the shows we watch have replaced the people our grandparents knew in those small towns and neighborhoods. We sometimes forget that these fictional families are not real. In real life, everybody doesn't hug at the end of the episode. In real life there's work that needs to be done. In real life, the toilets need to be cleaned and the trash has to be taken out.

WALLY AND THE BEAV

Because our expectations are based on fiction, we all think it is unfair that we have to do this kind of work. We don't see the television families doing it. They mostly just have fun. Why do we have to do it? This part of television hasn't changed, but the way the fictional TV families behave has! Your parents' generation had the expectation that a "nuclear family" was the ticket. (This was a term coined to indicate a mother, a father, and 2.6 children living in the same household.) The expectation of your parents came from the television they saw as they were growing up (now conveniently available on the cable network Nick@Night). The expectation of your parents' generation was that families should be like those portrayed in *The Donna Reed Show*, *Father Knows Best*, or *Leave it to Beaver*. You should watch some of these shows to get a feel for them. Even though your parents' families were nothing like these, they still got this picture in their head. You are part of a later generation, so you watch different shows, and your expectations are that families should be more like those in *Married with Children*, *Malcolm in the Middle*, *The Simpson's*, or *The Osborn's*. You're being Bud Bundy, Malcolm, or Bart, while you parents are expecting Wally and The Beaver. You see Bud or Malcolm's mom, and your mom wants to be Donna Reed. This is where we all get confused. None of us are these fictional characters.

These miracle families (either now or then) never had any real problems and devoted their time in each episode to Wally's first fender-bender, or the untimely visit by a slightly eccentric relative, Al Bundy sneaking off to the "nudie" bar, or Homer's latest "get rich quick" scheme. The houses your parents grew up in hardly resembled the place where June Cleaver lived, and your house is not Malcolm's.

Your parents still don't have Donna Reed's house, and they don't have a good set of family rules (experience from real people) to rely on. They're forced to make it up as they go along, and Donna Reed never had to face a drive-by shooting, elementary school sex, or the proliferation of newly fatal drugs and diseases (such as Ecstasy and AIDS). Toss in the fact that both parents now need to work to support a household and there are skyrocketing divorce rates, alcohol and drug addictions, and this leaves your generation with a sizable number of pretty dysfunctional families on their hands!

It is important to be aware of this historical perspective because families are a continuum stretching back literally to the beginning of time. Families have long histories and a lot of baggage gets handed down from generation to generation. You can understand a lot about your parents and the way your family is today by understanding what it was like for them and their parents when they were kids.

Teenagers want everyone to see things from their perspective. Taking a moment to see life from your parents' perspective is a big step in seeing the value of a family and the value you can get from it. Remember, parents are people too! Parents and families are not perfect; everyone has a lot of problems. Your job, your contributions to your family currency, can be measured by whether you make these problems a little better or a little worse. Are you helping things or hurting things? What contribution are you making? There's a saying "a rising tide raises all boats equally." This means that improving circumstances are good for everyone. Doing a little more family work makes the whole family better and a better place for you too!

YOU CAN'T PUSH A ROPE

Using your family well, getting the most out of it that you can, comes down to doing your part in making it as strong as it can be. This is about putting some time into the work of a family and enjoying the security it can provide. Family is the great safety net in life. This is about seeing things from your parents' and siblings' perspective, and thinking about that Christmas dinner when you're 35. Really trying to contribute to your family has a huge pay off, and that pay off will always come when you need it most. This is not just about money and help and getting you out of jams. The most valuable thing you can get from your family, no matter what its condition, is advice!

Not only do teenagers hate advice, it also seems like that is all anyone is ever interested in giving them. They hate advice because they are so busy trying to show everyone how capable they are, how they know how to do everything ("Look Ma, no hands!"). Somehow there's the feeling that if you listen to advice (even if you don't take it), you are somehow less capable, less able to do things on your own. This is the most idiotic thought that virtually all teenagers have. This is the biggest thing you have to get over in order to learn how to use your family successfully.

Advice is the most precious commodity on the planet. The people who consistently make the most money and who are in the most demand are people who give advice. Doctors, lawyers, accountants, contractors, consultants, and architects are all paid huge sums of money for their advice. They tell people what they should do. The president of the United States has the Executive Office Building, which houses thousands of staff members whose only job is to give him advice! The thing about advice, is that, like the president, the one accepting it is still responsible for the decision. You never see him saying that it was really this guy or that guy that gave him bad advice. Your success, anyone's success, is based on the decisions they make—using the advice they have received. The better your advice, the better your decisions will be. This is all part of finding out what you need to know!

It's a great skill to learn how to get and take advice, how to "use" other people's perspective and experience. Far from lessening your "bigness," your own capabilities, getting and taking good advice increases your maturity (how big you *really* are). This is where families really shine, and without question, you will get the most use out of them! They can provide very valuable advice, and they provide it for free!

My Guy

My parents hated Steven, I mean they really hated him. He got in a lot of trouble and was dealing drugs, but I wanted to be with him, and I guess I wanted to be in trouble too. I was always good, and I guess I wanted to be a bad girl too. He started out all nice and everything to me. He made me stuff. He didn't buy it, he made it—like collages with poems in them, and I really loved those things. At first my parents didn't really care so much, but when he started hanging out more, I guess they got to know more about him.

It was kind of weird, because I had boyfriends and stuff, and my parents knew them, but after a while, things would just kind of fizzle out, and they'd be gone. It was like that. So with Steven, when I guess things would have just started to fizzle, like he stopped making things, and started being kind of mean, I probably would have just let it go away, but my parents started really hating him and telling me I couldn't see him.

So that was really weird too, because even though he was mean and stuff, the more my parents told me to stay away from him, the more I wanted to be with him. So, it just went on and on. First, I was grounded from seeing him, but I saw him anyway, and then they took my car away. It seems like the more they did, the more I wanted to see him. It was really weird. So, finally, my parents were so mad, they sent me all the way to New Orleans to be with my real dad. I mean, that was so weird, I just got like sent away to New Orleans, and I'm just sitting there on the couch watching TV. I sat on the couch and watched TV for a whole month, and finally I got to come home.

So, I get home, and I'm still seeing Steven, and my parents are still hating him, and we're all just fighting all the time, and it's really horrible and I was going to just run away. So, anyway, at school they had this religious retreat thing, and my parents are begging me to go, so I went, I mean anything to just get out of there.

So, I'm at the retreat, and it's kind of horrible too, but one night there were just five of us, and we're talking, and we start to just let everything out, everything that's wrong. I start talking and telling these total strangers that I didn't need some guy to fulfill my life, and that I can't wait for someone else to make me happy, that I have to make myself happy, and it really made me think about everything I had done. I guess I sort of found myself. I found that I really only needed me, and not a whole bunch of people telling me stuff, telling me so much stuff I couldn't hear myself. So, I got home and dumped Steven, and really started to think about my parents because they were right, and to listen to them a little more, and not think they're just telling me to do stuff. They were really just trying to help, but I couldn't listen.

Alexis—20

A SUPPORT REPORT

No matter what you may think about them, family members can be very helpful in figuring out how to deal with life, and you can be helpful to them. This is a big part of the family currency idea. Even though you may think that your parents don't have a clue, anyone who's been wandering around on this planet for almost fifty years has a lot of experience to draw on, and anyone would be stupid not to take advantage of it. As Richard Pryor once said, "There's no such thing as an old fool, because you don't get old by being no fool!"

The best way to use a family is to *use* this advice. You don't have to *take* the advice, but a different perspective may help you to think more clearly about whatever issue you are facing. Paying attention to advice—hell, asking for it in the first place—is a great way to build up family currency. You're letting someone know that you care about their opinion. This makes them feel good, and they try really hard to do the best for you they can. Your family members are typically the only ones in your life who have no axe to grind when it comes to providing an opinion. They want what's best for you, because they may need to draw on some of *your* currency some day. They know they'll be at all of those Christmas dinners, too, and except in rare circumstances, they will not want you to think they screwed you over.

When you look at blood being thicker than water, you should now be seeing the huge and important impact families can have, and seeing the role you can play to make it so. You should be seeing your responsibility, your obligation to helping your family along. You're a link in a very long chain. You have to support your family so that they can support you, and this will be of great help when you are starting your own family! This is what a family should be about, not what you see on television. Families are about work and time. It takes a fair amount of both to keep them going.

Be involved! Care about what's going on with your parents and their lives. (It's funny to me that most teenagers don't even really understand what their parents do for a living!) Care about your brothers and sisters. Think really hard about things you can do on your own to make things easier for everyone (without being told). Look around—it's your house too! See if things need to be picked up, cleaned, or put away. Be a part of your family. Be an asset, not a problem.

Ask for advice. Be available to give advice. The payback is huge! Don't live in your house like it's a hotel room. Don't just act like everything happens by magic. When you are asked to help, be damn glad there is someone there to ask you for help, and that you're there to be helpful. People without families would give their right arm for this opportunity.

Understand that no one is perfect, especially your parents or siblings. Appreciate what it takes to put food on the table (earning the money, shopping for the stuff, cooking it, cleaning it up). Appreciate what it takes to put the table there in the first place (the mortgage, the jobs, the stress, the obligations). Don't be a wecnie! Family is work—do your share, in fact, do *more* than your share! You play an integral role in the strength of your family, and the stronger it is, the more you will be able to lean on it when you need it.

"BUT CAPTAIN, WE NEED MORE POWER!"

Lastly, no matter how much you put into it, don't expect your family to be an ever-loving, wonderful fiction like we see on TV. Because family groups are so close (they live in the same house 24/7) there is a lot of conflict and difference of opinion. There are a lot of things that are not fair. Accept and deal with the inevitable downside of your family. Living together is tough. No one ever gets everything they want and nothing is ever perfect. Sometimes when I think of family, I think of one of the original episodes of the TV show *Star Trek*, where Captain Kirk and Spock fight to the bitter end in the "Vulcan Ring of Death." Being unable to escape the ring, they must fight until one of them is dead. This is just like a family, except a family has more members, more participants in their own self-fashioned "Vulcan Ring of Death" (without the death, of course). I see this picture because the bonds of a family, the ties that make it such an inescapable and often hostile environment, are as equally based on negative human drives as they are on the positive ones—the love, caring, and compassion. These negative drives get a very good chance to work in a family. We have very long periods of time in which to foster and remember all the real and imagined injustices we've been served. Most discussions about families conveniently ignore this side, but its a big part of the reality. Forget about Donna Reed! Think of Kirk and Spock too!

Greed is the ever-present engine driving a family ("Who took the last cookie?" "Why's Tommy's slice bigger?" "Suzie got a bike, and I just got this crummy…") We want to think that families and parents are like Solomon, all wisdom, justice, and fairness. They're not! They're just regular people. Sometimes someone gets more, sometimes someone gets less. Pretty much everything evens out in the wash, as they say. Think about how "greedy" you are (or you sound) when you are the one saying all this stuff! Be generous. Be mature. Understand that over time you will get yours. Don't be a baby!

If greed is the engine, then guilt is the "nuts and bolts" that holds a family together. Guilt is how parents and siblings extract what they want from you. Guilt is the result of past greed. When someone is making you feel guilty, understand that they're really not *making* you do anything. You're the one making *yourself* feel guilty, and you do so because you feel you should. If you were perfect, you would never feel any guilt or remorse. It's OK—don't expect to be perfect. Expect to be guilty. You will have many, many things to feel guilty about. As you start to get this idea through your head, you will find that slowly (very slowly) you will begin to not do so many things that ultimately make you feel guilty. No one likes guilt, it's an angry, nasty rumbling in your belly. Learn to take your medicine. When you screw up (and you will!) there will be consequences, and your family is right there to dish them out. They are teaching you how to avoid guilt. They are teaching you to be a stand-up person. Admit when you've done them wrong, 'fess up, and accept the consequences. Whoosh, the guilt goes away!

So, if greed is the engine and guilt is the nuts and bolts, then resentment is the festering rust that's eating away at the under-carriage of every family. Resentment is like a pressure cooker. It grows and grows silently like cancer and then blows when we least expect it. It is the proverbial straw that breaks the camel's back. The "fertilizer" for growing resentment is the sense that we are owed something (like in the first section—the free lunch). We all value things differently. In your mind, buying a lollipop for your little sister is equal payment for her not telling your parents that *you* were the one who broke your mom's vase. But in her mind, you still owe her. When she attempts to extract more payment for her silence, you resent her for being greedy. When you don't pay up, she forgets about the lollipop and rats you out. She resents you for being selfish! When your mom finds out about the vase, she resents you for breaking it *and* for lying to her. She makes you feel guilty and punishes you too! She resents your dad for not being home when it happened because he was playing golf. He resents her for wanting him to do what he considers "her" job. Around and around we go. What do you expect? This is how all families (really all groups, for that matter) work.

Months later, your little sister needs a favor and you remem-ber the vase. (After all, you didn't get to go to the basketball game because you were grounded.) You tell her, "No way!" You add for good measure, "You rotten little snitch!" She resents you, and when you need some construction paper for your science project, she says "No way!" You go to your mom, and she resents both of you because now the construction paper crisis has pulled her away from the conclusion to *Law and Order*. She gets you the paper, and then yells at your dad for not putting his clothes in the laundry hamper. He resents you, he resents your sister, he resents your mom, and he probably resents *Law and Order*. Do you see how it works? Do you get the "resentment game"? The thing is—it is so easy to stop. Be bigger than they are. Who really cares anyway? Do your sister the favor. Lighten up! Be a help to your family. Look at the situation and really ask yourself why it's so important to always throw gasoline on the fire. Why be so stupid all the time? (Because they are?) Get real! Do you really want everyone to be laughing about what a jerk you used to be when you're at that Christmas dinner?

The fire extinguisher for resentment is appreciation. If someone is resenting you or you're resenting them, throw a little appreciation on it and the resentment will go away. When your sister wouldn't give you the construction paper, you started to fight with her. If instead you just stopped for a minute, looked at her, and told her how much you appreciated something that she had done for you in the past, you would see the resentment vanish. You may have to try this a few times because appreciation is so unusual and bizarre in a family that at first it may appear to be some kind of trick and raise suspicions. Anyway, you'd get the paper, your mom would see the action packed conclusion to *Law and Order*, and the whole cycle would never get a chance to start. Food for thought! This is what I mean by being an *asset* instead of a problem.

* * *

Key Points

So, you have an obligation to your family, but the big deal is *their* obligation to you. They are a group you can never leave, and they are the only one's who will be able and willing to provide the support you are going to need. Families have a good will bank account system, and you've got to make deposits to get withdrawals. This banking of good will currency has really big payoffs. Remember, every family has "legs" that extend beyond your immediate family. Think about the spheres of influence. Think about the gravitational center. Think about the strongest branch supporting your family tree and where your sprout is going to take the family into future generations. Never forget that horrible things are going to happen to you in life. Learn to separate family "reality" from all the screwy expectations people get from television. Don't let fictional characters become your role models. Think about the role model *you* are becoming. Appreciate and value everyone's different perspectives. Ask yourself often whether you are making things better or worse. For God's sake, ask for advice and value the opinions of others! Roll it around in your head and let it help you make decisions. This is ultimately best for you! Last, but not least, remember that it's not just all the goodie-two-shoes stuff when it comes to families. Understand the greed, guilt, and resentment factors. Pay attention. Be there for your family so they will be there for you!

* * *

You should now spend a little time talking about this:

- What do you think about your obligations to and from your family?
- What do you think are some of the things you will need from your family in the future?
- What do you think will be served at that Christmas dinner when you're 35?
- Where do you think this dinner will be held?
- Can you describe the spheres of influence in your family?
- Where's your family's gravitational center?
- What do you think is going to happen with your branch of the family tree?
- Do you understand how TV may have screwed up your expectations?
- Do you understand how important good advice is?
- Do you think other family members have valuable opinions, perspectives, and experiences?

fat, drunk, and stupid is no way to go through life, son!

This section is titled with a quote from the movie *Animal House*. The dean of the college is threatcning a few of the guys from the frat house he hates and offers this line as advice. It is very good advice. This section is mostly about the drunk and stupid parts. This section is about sex, drugs, and rock and roll (but not really so much the rock and roll). To save a little time, I'll use the term "sex" to primarily mean premarital, underage sex. Likewise, I will use the word "wasted" to indicate the effects of *all* drugs and alcohol. Sex and getting wasted go together because they are about the same thing—getting off, the physical release of endorphins, hormones that make you feel good.

Here is where you expect to hear how bad all this stuff is, and why you should avoid it like the plague. But like Epictetus said, things are neither "good" nor "evil" of their own accord; it's only our use of them that makes them one or the other. (Guns don't kill people. People kill people.) One person may use marijuana as a remedy for glaucoma or as an appetite enhancer to help combat the side effects of cancer or AIDS. Another may use it just to get screwed up. It's the use and the intent that you need to pay attention to here. This includes sex. You need to be thinking about how this stuff fits into your plan, your direction in life. Is getting laid or wasted going to get you closer to your goal or further away? Is it better to do, not to do, and when? Is it just a distraction? It's your call, but this stuff is important enough that you should at least consider all the various consequences and repercussions. This section is about what you intend to get out of getting screwed up and what to watch out for.

LET'S PARTY!

Sex, drugs, and rock and roll have become sort of a right of passage in our culture, and this makes the intent part of it kind of confusing. Throughout history, most cultures and religions have developed ceremonies to officially welcome a teenager into the world of adulthood (bar mitzvah, confirmation, "bridging," Testimony, and even debutante balls). The culmination of these ceremonies always involves *rights* and *obligations*. Our culture has kind of left the "obligation" side in the dust. Getting a driver's license, being able to vote or join the army, being able to purchase cigarettes or alcohol—all have all become our culture's rights of passage, our new ceremonies (in a very consumer-driven society).

Your twenty-first birthday marks your ability to purchase alcohol in most states, and this seems to be the last thing necessary to becoming an adult. It's traditionally celebrated by getting wasted. Not only has no one really talked to you about the responsibilities that go along with drinking (the obligation part), but your first practical lesson is to learn how to be as irresponsible as you can! We like the *rights*, but we forgot about the *obligations*. It's like the chicken and the egg—what comes first? It used to be that you would go through a process (learning) and a ceremony (bar mitzvah, confirmation), and *then* you were eligible for the rights (you were considered well versed in the obligations that go with the rights). Now, the rights (getting laid or wasted) seem to have become the ceremony—because you "can," you "should"!

This is screwed up! These "ceremonies" have evolved in a kind of vacuum with very little attention paid to the consequences or repercussions (obligations and knowledge) that should go with them—driving at 16, losing your virginity at the senior prom, or drinking at 21. The "obligations" that go along with these events involve responsibility, and unfortunately, only with driving does our culture demand that you be prepared—you have to get a license and pass a course. And, just like driving a car, you also have the responsibility to not harm yourself or others when you're having sex or getting wasted. The law says you are officially old enough to do this stuff, and the question becomes whether you are officially "responsible" enough to really understand all the repercussions and obligations. Driving a car irresponsibly can kill you or someone else. So can sex and getting wasted. Too bad there isn't a "driver's education" program for sex and getting wasted (both written and behind the wheel, so to speak).

Ask Alice

I did a lot of drugs, mostly meth. I would never have imagined it starting because I was on the honor roll and didn't hang out with the kids that were into drugs. I guess if I really had to point to a cause, I'd have to say that it was *because* I was doing well in school. Because of this, my parents gave me a car when I was 17, and since I had already taken most of the harder classes, my school schedule was pretty slim. Although everything was going smoothly, I didn't really feel all that good about myself. I knew I was smart and pretty funny, but I didn't really feel like I fit in anywhere. I was one of those "in between" people. I was smart enough to take classes with the nerds, but just a little too popular to really hang out with them. I was sort of "second level" popular, not the jock-cheerleader kind of popular. I always knew where all the parties were, but I was never really in the middle of things. I was always just watching people have fun, and never really having fun with them. It was kind of complicated.

So, summer came along. It was the summer between junior and senior year. My friends and I started going to the beach a lot, and it was just like the parties. We were kind of on the outer edge of the inner circle. I started to feel a little more confident as my tan deepened and my hair got lighter from the sun. The exercise helped too.

One day, this boy Duncan came up to me at the beach, and asked me if I'd like to go to a party with him on Saturday. Duncan was really cute, and very cool. I was thrilled. That night I went to the mall with my friends and picked up this beautiful sun dress for the party. When I tried it on, and looked in the changing-room mirror, I saw a very pretty, popular girl looking back at me.

Duncan picked me up on Saturday and we went to the party. It was pretty wild, and I was having so much fun. It was like everyone kept coming up to us and joking and telling us how good we looked together. I was in heaven, and felt so special. We were standing by the pool talking to some of Duncan's friends and Tommy lit up a joint. I'd never smoked before, and was immediately very nervous. Tommy handed the joint to Duncan. He took a hit, looked at me, and said, "Alice, you're so sweet and wonderful, I'm sure you've never done this before, so just take a little, or you don't have to at all." That was such a nice thing to do, to be so gallant, and take the pressure off. It made me feel so connected to him that I wanted to do it for him, if that makes any sense. Anyway the joint went around a few times, I got a pretty good buzz, and the party really took off. I guess Duncan and I kind of fell in love that night. It was magic.

So, we were pretty inseparable from then on. We'd smoke at the beach and it was just like the party, so much fun. As time went on, we did some coke and ended up making love. By the end of the summer, Duncan and I were pretty much high all the time, and had started doing meth quite a bit. At first, we'd just do a little at parties if someone offered it to us. Then we started buying. Pretty soon, we stopped going to the beach, and would just go and party at whoever's house during the day. My tan faded, and it was like we could never quite get enough. We'd sit around for hours talking nonsense. We'd mostly talk about how screwed up everything and everybody was.

School started, and we just kept on going. Somehow or other I'd become a "tweaker." I started fighting with my parents, ditching classes, and just doing as much meth as I could get my hands on.

A couple of months into the term, I stopped at a mini-mart to get some gas for my car. I was going inside to pay just as Cindy and Melanie were coming out. They used to be my best friends. When I saw them I felt really nervous and self-conscious. They said hi, and Cindy asked me if I was OK. That made me mad. OK? What was this mousy little nerd saying to me! I went off on her. I don't really know what I said, but I was yelling, and finally, she just grabbed my shoulders, spun me around, and held me in front of the big plate glass window of the mini-mart. She was screaming in my ear, "Look at you, look what you've become!"

Well, I kind of froze there, and saw myself for the first time in a long time. Cindy and Melanie walked to their car, and I just stood there looking at myself. What happened to that girl in the sun dress? I was thin and pale, my clothes were a mess, my hair stringy and dirty. My face was drawn, and my eyes looked dead. I started to cry. I was crying so hard, that the guy who worked there came out and asked me what was going on. I ran to my car and drove straight home. I went to my Mom, still bawling my eyes out. I told her I needed to go to rehab.

That was about a year ago, and I've been clean ever since. I tried to get Duncan to go, but we just had a big fight and that was the end of it for us. What I realized was that getting high made you think that you were so on top of everything, and the world was what was so screwed up. Getting high was supposedly making you see everything so much clearer, but really, it was just the opposite. Being high was not making you see *anything* clearer; it was just making you not see yourself. The world wasn't so screwed up, you were! In the end, it's not how you see the "out there" that matters so much, but how you see the "in here" that really counts.

Alice—19

READY, WILLING, AND ABLE

Just because the law has set certain ages as the time when they consider most people responsible enough to figure out the obligation part all on their own, there's still a fairly sizable group who are not responsible enough, even though they've had the legal number of birthdays. Worse yet, there's another sizable group that can't even seem to wait for these rather lenient dates.

There are a whole bunch of people out there doing this stuff, a lot who are not ready, whether they've reached the legal age or not! It's these people you need to watch out for. They will get you in trouble. They have already started down a rocky path and they want to take as many people with them as they can. Beware the dark side, Luke. It's really not that this stuff will absolutely ruin your life, although it can. It's just that invariably, this stuff is an obstacle, it makes it harder to get and keep what you really should be wanting in life.

It's not about how old you are; it's about how ready you are to deal with it. Age or the law should have very little to do with it. The only thing that should matter to you is *you*! This stuff is important and dangerous enough that it's worthwhile to really understand the obligations that go with it. Take a hard look at your seven or eight inches. You'll have plenty of time for this stuff, and I promise you that it's a whole lot more fun when you do it right! So, the Life Lesson here is that there is no real "good" or "bad" or "if" to sex or getting wasted—it's all about "when." When are *you* going to be ready? (Hint: It has nothing to do with your age.)

Think about it this way. Let's imagine a fictional kid. This kid's father is huge, say six feet ten inches and three hundred pounds. Let's say his mom is too. He's probably one of the biggest kids in his class and will be a very big guy when he's an adult. We'll add that he is also unbelievably coordinated, a natural athlete. It would be fair to say that this kid has an excellent chance of being a professional football player—he's big, quick, and coordinated. Now, let's imagine him at age 17 when he's almost as physically big as he's going to get. He decides to go tryout with the Oakland Raiders football team. He will get the crap kicked out of him! This is not a presumption—this is a fact! Why? Even though he has everything going for him to do this successfully one day, today ain't his day! He's just not ready. He isn't fully "cooked" yet!

He's not going to get much bigger, or necessarily stronger, but the reason he gets the crap kicked out of him is because he's not mentally or emotionally "tough" enough to deal with it. This includes his ability to deal with nerves, stress, pressure, confidence, insecurities, and self esteem. Having a good handle on this emotional and mental stuff takes time and experience—and there's no substitute. Just like the kid with the Raiders, it's exactly the same for you with sex and getting wasted. Although your body may be ready, your ability to think about it the right way may not be (the nerves, confidence, insecurities, and self esteem stuff). When you're not both physically and mentally prepared for something, you invariably get the crap kicked out of you. This is a Fact of Life.

ALL WORK AND NO PLAY MAKES JACK A DULL BOY

So, why are you so driven? Why are sex, drugs, and rock and roll such powerful magnets? Teenagers are very gung-ho to be adults, to prove how "big" they are. It's a weird kind of limbo. Your body becomes adult far before your brain does, and sometimes you forget that the brain is the part that really matters. So in this somewhat mindless dash to be "big," we get the cause and effect all mixed up—"If I do adult stuff, I therefore become an adult." This is part of it. Sex and getting wasted seem to be very "adult" things, and you want to be an adult.

Another reason is that sex and getting wasted are plastered throughout the media. From magazine racks to virtually every commercial message you see, sex and getting wasted are what it's all about! Let's party! Next, you're also drawn to this stuff because you are not "supposed" to. This is the taboo/desire/rebellion side. "Well, I'll show you!"

With sex in particular, there's also a physical side to it. Your body has been designed by thousands of years of evolution to want to make babies as soon as you possibly can (caused by hormones which are very, very potent chemicals).

Lastly, there's the mystery, the curiosity of the unknown. Our society is not very good at passing along the right information about this stuff, and there's a drive to simply find out for ourselves.

Probably the biggest reason you are drawn to these things is that you think they're a lot of fun. This is true. Sex and getting wasted are a lot of fun. They make you feel really, really good. So, the first lesson about the *obligations* (repercussions/consequences) is to get a handle on what's drawing you to sex and getting wasted. Is it to feel older, experience the taboo or mystery, simple body chemistry, or do you just want to have fun? What are you trying to accomplish, and is this the best or even the right way to go about it? This is the first thing to be thinking about. What's <u>really</u> making you want to do this stuff? Peer pressure?

ON YOUR MARK, GET SET…

Sex, having an orgasm, is a great feeling. Getting wasted can also be a great feeling. Sex is a great feeling because our brains are programmed for it—it's hardwired into our circuitry. Getting wasted is a great feeling because it "short-circuits" the hardwired parts of the brain that control our actions. We do things we normally wouldn't do. (Getting wasted even comes with its own built-in excuse: "Man I was so screwed up I didn't know what I was doing!")

So let's say you really know why you want to get laid or get wasted, you're OK with it, and that somehow you're convinced it fits in with your plan in life. How do you know whether you're really ready? You will be ready when you understand *all* the obligations and consequences. It should be just like passing the written and driving tests at the DMV, where you prove you understand all the obligations and repercussions of driving. You need to think about getting laid or wasted the same way. Could you pass the test? What would be on the test?

One thing to know for sure is that, especially when you're a teenager (or even into adulthood for some), you are very, very bad at figuring out consequences on your own (if *this* is what I do, *that* will most likely happen). Consequences are the link between what you do and what you get. If a certain action has five possible outcomes (each with their own set of consequences), a teenager will invariably see only three out of the five. This is because of your lack of experience. It's nothing to feel bad about. It just is. You simply haven't been on the planet long enough to consider all the possible outcomes. Be honest with yourself and accept this Fact of Life too!

You will probably be well into your twenties before you start to get very good at predicting consequences. How many times have you had things not turn out the way you planned? How many times has something totally unexpected foiled your scheme? Probably a lot! How often are you surprised by life? ("I didn't see *that* coming!") This is the real measurement of your maturity (how good you are at figuring out the probable consequences of your actions). Sex and getting wasted have a whole bunch of consequences. With these things, the unexpected is never a pleasant surprise! You are ready for this stuff when you've found that you haven't been surprised by life for a decent period of time. That's when you'll know you are fully "cooked," when you'll know you are a real adult (physically, mentally, and emotionally). Some people *never* get there.

SEX WITHOUT LOVE IS A MEANINGLESS EXPERIENCE, BUT AS FAR AS MEANINGLESS EXPERIENCES GO…

Sex is a primal drive that cuts through virtually everything in our lives. You're familiar with the obvious consequences. You hopefully know about getting pregnant and catching STDs (sexually transmitted diseases), some of which can kill us. There are several forms of birth control that keep us from getting pregnant although *none* are perfect. Condoms can block the STDs, but these are not perfect either. Therefore, when it comes to sex, no matter how careful you are, a potential consequence is always pregnancy and disease. There are oral and manual alternatives to intercourse, and these are pretty effective, though should not necessarily be considered "safer" when it comes to the transmission of STDs. Although it's critical to know about this stuff, the biggest mistake that's usually made, the biggest unexpected consequence, is not realizing what a powerful freight train sex can be! In the heat of passion, once the ball gets rolling, your brain checks out. While your plan was to do this and that to protect yourself and your partner, these plans are often left on the floor with your Levi's and forgotten intentions. This is probably the biggest "unexpected" surprise! Be prepared. Sex is like an avalanche. Once it gets started it's very hard to apply the brakes.

Sex

OK, this is just so totally weird to be talking about, but, OK, I mean, whatever. Anyway, I'm like a pretty good girl and all that, I mean about sex and stuff. I mean, like I've done oral, well, you know, a couple of times, and it was kind of, like, no big deal, but anyway, whatever. So there's this party and a bunch of us go and everything, and there's like music, and people are dancing, and there's beer and everything, we're just all partying and stuff. I guess I had a few beers or something, and it's really fun and everything, and there's this really hot guy, I mean, he's really cute.

So we're all talking, and I'm pretty drunk, and he says he's got some smoke in his jacket, so we go back in the house to this room. He gets this roach from his jacket, and we light it up. We're just back there and talking and stuff. Anyway, I guess it was the pot or something, but I'm like way high, and we're talking, and he starts kissing me and stuff, and I'm like kissing him too.

So there's like this big couch back there, and pretty soon we're on it, and we're kissing and holding each other, and it's just so hot. So anyway, we're like really into it, and things are going really fast, and I'm kind of, whatever, and pretty soon, like some of our clothes are off and everything. We're there, and we start to do it, and I'm all like, "What are you doing!" He's like, "Oh, uh," and I'm all like, "You need a condom," and he's all like, "OK, OK," and I guess he had one or something, so we did it. I felt really weird, like, this wasn't the way I pictured it at all! So, anyway, I like didn't tell anybody about this. Well, I told Carla, and she's like my best friend and everything. So, like a couple weeks goes by, and all of the sudden I've got this pain, I mean, it's all, well, itchy and stuff, and I talk to Carla, and she's all like, "You got to go to a doctor" and everything, and I'm all like, "No way," but it just kept going on and everything.

Anyway, me and Carla go to this clinic place, and I get this examination, and we have to wait for them to call with the results, and we're all afraid someone's going to find out. So the call comes, and they tell me I got this stuff chlamydia or something, and I've never even heard of it. I mean, I've heard of VD and stuff, but not this.

So, I ask them what it is, and they tell me about it and everything, and tell me I need all these antibiotics. So, I'm thinking about the sex, and how it hardly happened, I mean, how it just barely happened before he put the condom on. Just basically a few seconds, and now I've got to take these antibiotics, and it's like really painful, and, like, what was I thinking anyway? It just all happened so fast and everything. Anyway, now I've got to try and find this guy and let him know what's going on because he needs the antibiotics too, and like, I don't know, it's just like such a bust. I mean, I was thinking that I'd always remember my first time and all that, and I, well, I guess I will, but this isn't how I thought it was going to be.

Veronica-17

Another "unexpected" surprise, and one of the biggest consequences of sex, is the emotions. Sex is one of the most intimate things you can do with another person. No matter what the drive, no matter what the circumstances, no matter what the intent, having sex with someone creates a lot of very powerful emotions. These emotions are not about the "love," as in, "Oh baby, oh baby, I 'love' you so much!" These are deeper emotions that are harder to see. They're about how you begin to see yourself and your partner(s) in a sexual context. I would guess that about half of all the money spent on therapy is due to this "unexpected" surprise.

Men and women have very different attitudes when it comes to sex, love, and intimacy. A lot of these attitudes come from the media. Most men see sex as a casual, fun byproduct of a relationship. Most women see sex in relation to a level of commitment. These two views are at odds with one another. While men often consider sex casually as "no big deal," simply "getting off," women usually see it as a much bigger deal. This is slowly changing, but the consequences are huge. The attitudes you learn about dealing with sex have an enormous impact on your ability to have and sustain relationships for your whole life. For a big part of your seven or eight inches, you are going to be involved in relationships, so this is important. The trap between these two views (which is highly reinforced in the media and pornography in particular) is that women are simply seen as objects for sex, and this has a lot of negative repercussions. Since guys are almost always ready, willing, and able, girls have become the "gate-keepers" of sex (both literally and figuratively). As the gate-keepers, they're what's "needed" to have sex, thereby becoming the sexual object. It's really a lot more complicated than that, but for now, this should get the concept across.

TWO VIEWS

For women, learning (incorrectly) to see themselves as objects creates a whole host of problems. First and foremost, they become obsessed with their appearance. After all, an object is only known by what it looks like. Since very few people have the looks or body of the ever-present supermodel, they begin a lifelong process of reconstruction that, more often than not, ends in frustration. Secondly, and perhaps of more concern, women begin to view their sexuality in relation to their desirability as an object. This is the "He will only 'love' me if I have sex with him" syndrome. Both of these not-so-obvious consequences lead to unhappiness. Both consequences can be eliminated by simply being aware of what's going on. A little bit of clear thinking here can do away with a lifetime of unnecessary distress. Women need to think long and hard about how they see themselves in this context. Your early experience with this stuff sets the pattern for your whole life. Women need to see themselves as whole partners and whole people, not just as a sex toy. Men need to stop playing on that insecurity.

For men, learning to see women as objects creates a whole host of different problems. Here, men learn to see women as "prey," the "can I get in her pants" syndrome. This view of women will keep you from ever enjoying a truly satisfying relationship. With the emphasis on "conquest," you can never really accept a woman as an equal partner and will miss a part of life that is much better than the sex. Sure, you "get off" going from woman to woman, but the longer it goes on, the less fulfilling it becomes, and eventually you will be unable to connect with women in any other way than a few minutes of far-less-than meaningful sex. Here, too, the remedy to this potential consequence is just having your eyes open. What are you really trying to accomplish—the sex or a partnership? Many times the answer is just the sex, but the problem surfaces when you want a partner and no longer have the ability to see women as anything more than a sex toy. Men have to think about their view of women and how this affects their ability to be a real man. Real men don't "possess" or "conquer" a woman. Real men see a woman as a necessary and valuable partner in the very difficult journey of life.

These two sets of consequences that come from both men's and women's views of sex have populated the bar and singles scene of our culture with a vast wasteland of men seeking women whom they have no real desire to have a relationship with, and women who fit the bill. This is another unexpected surprise (or consequence) of sex—seeing people as individuals (as whole people, as Shakespeare wrote, "If I am pricked, do I not bleed?"), and understanding that it is the *relationship* that should really be the goal. Sex is just a fun fringe benefit! This is how you should think about sex.

PSSST…OVER HERE

Now let's talk about how you should think about getting wasted. This is a little trickier in that there are no "basics" to getting wasted like there are with sex (contraception, prevention of STDs, and so on). Getting wasted is also a primal drive. The stress, problems, and anxiety of day to day life take their toll. A few hours of relief is a welcome opportunity.

Since we don't necessarily have a good set of basics when it comes to getting wasted, I'll provide it. There are four categories of things that can get you wasted.

Natural	Prescription	Processed	Designer
cigarettes	amphetamines	cocaine	MDA
alcohol	barbiturates	heroin	ecstasy
marijuana	pain relievers	opium	PCP
mushrooms	mood altering	glue	narcozep or "date rape"
peyote	miscellaneous	amyl nitrate	GHB
			LSD
			meth amphetamine

There are a lot more, but you get the general idea here. *All* of these, and many more, are addicting. ALL! This is a Fact of Life. Some may be more so than others. Some may cause a psychological addiction, while others are totally physical. Lesson one on intoxicants—*all* are addicting, and this is the first consequence you are likely to experience. If something makes you feel good, either your brain or your body is going to want to do it again ("I've been smoking pot for twenty years, and I ain't addicted!).

The list above is arranged somewhat in order of potential dangers. "Natural" drugs are not good for you like "natural food." They are labeled as such because there's not a lot of processing that goes on. "Prescription" drugs are next, and while they are prescribed by doctors for specific ailments, they can be very dangerous when used in combination, or if you have certain medical conditions that you might not even be aware of, or if you get the dosage wrong. "Processed" drugs are next, and about the only "good" thing you can say about them is that we have a pretty good understanding of their effects because they've been around for quite a while. "Designer" drugs are the most dangerous because they are relatively new and there's little understanding of the potential side effects. We really don't know everything they do yet.

So much for the basics. The biggest thing to understand about getting wasted (using any of the above) is that they all "short-circuit" your brain, and that's basically the point. You do this stuff so that your brain doesn't work very well. The obvious consequence of this is that you are liable to do something really stupid. The primary function of your brain is to keep you out of trouble. When you take something that makes it malfunction, you are more likely to get into trouble, and that's why you are probably interested in getting wasted in the first place. Pretty simple stuff.

DRAIN BRAMAGE

A somewhat longer-lasting and potentially more dangerous consequence (an "unexpected" one) is that all this stuff has what's called a "cumulative effect." Each and every time you get wasted, you are doing a little damage to your brain that can never be repaired. Think about it like waves from the ocean slowly eroding a cliff. Each wave doesn't do that much, but over the years the cliff is toast! This is a Fact of Life, a guaranteed consequence of getting wasted.

Worse yet, there is a consequence to this consequence. It has to do with the condition of your boat (from section three). The world out there is a really, really competitive place. There's only so much stuff in the world (food, wealth, status, fame, and so on), and *everybody* is trying to get their hands on as much as they possibly can. It's kind of like everyone scrambling around underneath a giant piñata. To be thrown in with the sharks, you are going to need to have all your wits about you. Most people get clobbered by life even when they are fully "competitive"— as strong, sharp, clever, and nimble as they can possibly be. To purposely ingest something that makes you less competitive is a losing strategy. It is thrilling for those you would have been competing with because they now have one less person to deal with. It's like taking yourself out of the race, like taking an axe to the hull of your boat. If you were given a brand new Ferrari, I doubt that you would put sugar in the gas tank (knowing that this would ruin the engine). Every time you have anything to do with getting wasted, you are putting sugar in your own gas tank, knowing that this will eventually ruin your brain.

So you've thought about the consequences, and you're going to get wasted anyway! Pretty much everybody does. Just like the discussion on sex, the only thing you can try to do to avoid the dangerous consequences is be aware that they exist. Know what you're doing. Be aware of what you know and what you *don't* know. Drinking some vodka might be strongly addicting for you or maybe not, but at least you are pretty sure that it's just vodka. Doing some "blow" or taking

"X" may also present some problems, but here you're not even sure that it is what it's supposed to be ("Dude! Ricky says this is the kind!"). Understand that when you do any of this stuff, your brain will immediately begin to not work very well, and you are liable to do something you had no intention of doing (perhaps "other" intoxicants, driving, or having sex). Understand that you are not going to be thinking very well, and it's a good idea to be in as safe an environment as you can. It's one thing to smoke a joint at your friends house and watch MTV—it is entirely another thing to smoke a joint on a road trip to LA. Pay attention to what you intend to do while you still have the mental faculties to think it through. One weak moment of "Oh, what the hell" can have a lifelong, or life-ending, impact.

A BULLET OR A BOMB?

A key element to getting wasted with our "substance of choice" is *dosage*. How much should you take? All drugs affect people differently. Some people's metabolism makes them more resistant to the effect and other's do not. More or less, you can relate dosage to weight. A heavier person can handle more than a smaller one. How much you can handle seems to have become some sort of "macho" test ("That dude's such a lightweight")—and this is idiotic. I don't think you would want your doctor to have this attitude! All of this stuff gets absorbed into your body. It takes about half an hour for things you swallow to hit your blood stream. Things you inject or snort or smoke hit much faster. Expect a big lag between when you ingest something and when you feel all of the effects.

Poor Ian

Well, I'm from Chicago, and I did a lot of drugs in high school. I mean a lot! Coke, PCP, crack, meth, acid…a whole bunch of stuff. My best friend Ian and me started doing this stuff GHB. It's a body builder thing, kind of slows your muscles down or something and gets you high. So you drink this stuff, and twenty ounces is like $200, and you're only supposed to do a cap full, but me and Ian are just drinking it out of the bottle and screwing around working on our cars and stuff. So, this stuff is really bad news because it slows you down so much. So we're working on our cars and Ian just falls down in the dirt, and he's not breathing, and I feel for his pulse, and can't feel it, and it's just like his whole body just shut down.

So, I run and call the paramedics because I thought he was dead or something. They're like right there, and there's a bunch of cops, and I'm wondering if he's dead or not, but they get him breathing, and put him in the ambulance, and then the cops are all looking around, and they find a bunch of bottles of the stuff and arrest me. We both get arrested for possession with intent to distribute which is really heavy. The judge tells me that I have a choice to either go to prison or to get my shit together and join the military, so I join the Marines. Ian didn't get to do that because he had some priors, so he ended up getting five to ten years.

Anyway, I went to boot camp for three months, and it was just like one big huge detox for me, six days a week. On Sundays you could either hang with the drill instructors or go to church, so I went to a lot of church. There's still like a bunch of drugs around and everything, even though you're in the Marines, but with the camp and church, I guess I just wasn't into it anymore. Ian went to prison, and even though he could have got out in two and a half years, he got in some big hassle there, and now he's got to serve his full sentence. I got my record dropped, and haven't done any drugs for three years. I got married six months ago. Poor Ian.

John—22

If you are so driven to do this stuff, at least be smart about the way you do it. It's always easier to wait a little while and do more than to do too much and wish you hadn't. You should always let someone you trust (I mean *really* trust) know exactly what it is you think you are taking and *how much*! Drugs can very quickly make you unconscious or incoherent, and having someone who can tell a paramedic what's going on can save your life. IF SOMEONE, OR YOURSELF HAS A BAD REACTION TO SOMETHING, GET THEM TO AN EMERGENCY ROOM IMMEDIATELY. Don't be scared, or afraid of the cops, or any of that crap. *No problem with the police or the law or parents is EVER as big a problem as being dead!* Lastly, because most kids start getting wasted by drinking alcohol, here's a little tip. Understand that it takes about half an hour for the alcohol to go from your stomach to your blood stream. This means that however tipsy you feel at any given moment, you will get more so in half an hour without drinking any more! Feel your face. When your face feels numb, you're done!

✳ ✳ ✳

Key Points

So sex, drugs, and rock and roll are all about getting off. It's not so much about the "act" of doing it as the "intent." What do you expect to get out of the experience? Understand the obligations and don't let the false ceremonies of reaching a certain age force your hand. There are a whole lot of repercussions, and goofing around like this is just getting in the way of accomplishing your real goals. This stuff is a lot more fun when you do it right, and doing it right is all about being really ready— physically, mentally and emotionally! Think about why you are so driven. Is it to be "big"? Is it because of the media or the fact you're not supposed to, or hormones, or the mystery of the unknown? Is it because you just want to have fun? Whatever it is—is it really a good enough reason? Think about how bad you are at figuring out the consequences of your actions. Think about how often you are "surprised" by life. Think about how this is a measurement of your maturity.

Understand that sex can be like a freight train, and that there are a whole bunch of emotional consequences that last a lifetime. Think about how men and women think differently about sex and relationships. Beware of seeing women as objects. Understand that relationships should always be your goal, and learn to work at being good at this. Never forget that ALL intoxicants are addicting! Understand that what you're doing is "short-circuiting" your brain, and expect that it will not to work very well when you're wasted. Know that your brain will not do a very good job of keeping you out of trouble. Think about your competitiveness and what getting wasted does for it. If you are doing something, know what the hell it is. Don't just believe what someone else has to say about it. Know what you *don't* know! Always be thinking about dosage, and for God's sake, let someone you trust know what's going on. Think about what you're doing while you still have a fully functioning brain!

✳ ✳ ✳

You should now spend a little time talking about this:

- What do you think about your intentions with respect to sex and drugs?
- Do you think you have a good handle on obligations and repercussions?
- How physically, mentally, and emotionally mature do you really think you are?

- When was the last time you were "surprised" by life, by the unexpected?
- How do you feel about the emotional consequences of sex, its connection to relationships?
- Do you think all intoxicants are addicting?
- Do you see how your brain is going to react to getting wasted?
- Do you get how important it is to let someone know what you're doing?
- Are you responsible enough to get someone who's having trouble to the emergency room?

timing is everything!

(How to Be Lucky)

Well, we're almost done, and what better subject to end on than luck. Who doesn't want to be lucky? Luck makes up for a lot of shortcomings in life ("I'd rather be lucky than good!"). You don't have to be as smart as someone else, or as skilled, talented, or clever if you're lucky. Luck is really one of the most simple things, and it can be controlled. You can be as lucky as you want if you pay attention, if you are thinking. No matter how you define "luck," it always comes down to being at the *right place* at the *right time*. Perhaps of more importance is the counterintuitive side of this. Being "unlucky" is a matter of being in the *wrong place* at the *wrong time*! Simple as that. These two Facts of Life can have a huge impact on your life and what you get out of it. You can control where you are (the place), and you can control the time. The place is pretty clear cut, so we are going to deal mostly with the time in this section. Timing is everything!

DUMB LUCK

One of my favorite stories is of a business associate of mine, Ken, who ran a very important division of a very big company. Originally, Ken graduated from college and pretty much became a bum, wandering and partying around the country with absolutely no prospects of making a living or getting a job. He met a girl from Chicago while they were both vacationing in Florida. When she went home, he decided he needed to see her again, so he went to Chicago to find her, knowing only that she worked at this very big company. When he got there, he went to the corporate offices of this company and started wandering around the halls looking for her—not a particularly clever plan.

In one hallway, an executive came storming out of his office, looked at Ken, and asked him where the hell he had been. Ken had no idea what he was talking about, and the executive then told him where he should go to work and what he wanted done. The executive mistook Ken for someone else who was supposed to show up for work that day. A little bewildered, but with really nothing better to do, Ken went to the desk and started doing the work he was asked to do. Ken was with this company for eighteen years and made a ton of money. Ken was very lucky. Ken was at the right place at the right time. Unfortunately, Ken had no idea what he was doing, just looking for some girl, but he was presented with an opportunity and took it. This is what's called "dumb luck." By the way, he did find the girl—they got married and had kids.

It was dumb luck because there was no particular plan or thought that went into this. There was no way that someone could have predicted what would happen. It's just a funny story with a happy ending. Dumb luck happens all the time, and this is what most people think about when they think about *all* luck. But this is not what it's about. This kind of luck is just about odds. You can expect an equal amount of good "dumb luck" and bad "dumb luck" (dumb un-luck) to happen to you during your life. This stuff is totally out of your control. This is stuff happening to you as opposed to *you* happening to it. I'll come back to this, but first, I need to mention that you can even have some control over "dumb luck."

HIT ME!

Blackjack (sometimes called "21") is a fun card game. I suggest you learn how to play. It's fun because you gamble, but also because it can teach you a lot about controlling dumb luck. I won't go into all the rules here, but the point in this game is that if you play smart, you have better odds than the dealer, who has to take a card when they have sixteen and has to "stay" (not take a card) when they have seventeen. If you follow the same rules, you have exactly the same "odds" as the dealer (they will win 50 percent of time and you will win 50 percent of the time). This is one of the purest examples of dumb luck.

What's interesting about this game is that even though you are assured by the laws of probability (mathematical proofs) that you will win half the hands, you will *never* win every other hand. There are streaks. Sometimes you win five in a row, then the dealer wins thee, then you win one, then they win four—you get the picture. The reason you have "better" odds is because you don't *have* to follow the dealer's rules, and you don't *have* to bet the same amount of money on each hand. If you were able to bet $10 on the hands you won and only $5 on the hands you lost, you would end up with a very big pile of money.

Ah, the problem! How do you know which hands are which? You can't, and this is why Las Vegas has a whole lot more money than you do. People go there and they think they can tell when they'll win and when they'll lose. They lose all their money. There are a lot of theories to blackjack, and I won't dwell on the pros or cons of gambling, but the point here is that just like in blackjack, you are dealt certain hands to play every day (the stuff that does or doesn't happen to you). Just like in blackjack, the odds are 50/50 that they will be either good things or bad things. Just like in blackjack, if you have more money on the table for the good things, you will end up winning in life.

GOOD THINGS COME IN INFREQUENT PACKAGES

So, what am I talking about? You can have more money on the table in real life because you get to bet *after* you see your cards.

Certain things are going to happen every day, some good, some bad. You will know when it's a good or a bad thing. If you take advantage of the good things, really run with them, and try to immediately avoid the bad things, you are putting more money on the table for your winning hands.

Say a girl or a guy that you really want to meet flies around the corner of a hallway and bumps into you—a good thing! You have to be prepared to take advantage of this dumb luck—just like the guys in the kung fu movies who are always ready to whip out the nunchakus at a moment's provocation. You, too, need to be constantly ready to take advantage of any good dumb luck that comes your way. This bumping into someone is an opportunity to do what you desire, to get to know that person. Seize the day! Act! Put more money on the table! This is the time to gamble! This is a Fact of Life. The better you get at learning to take advantage of an opportunity, the better off you'll be.

Making Your Own Luck

I got lucky because I met Erica. We've been together about two years now. I was in school, and I was going to spend the summer in Europe, and that was going to be so cool. So, I'm in this English class, and I guess I kind of screwed it up, and I had to take summer school in order to graduate, and was so pissed because that screwed up my Europe trip and everything.

So summer school was almost over and I passed the English class, and my parents say they're going to Hawaii, and that I can go too. I'm kind of into that, but I'm still all pissed off and everything about Europe. So we get in this big fight, and I'm all like, "I'm out of here!" so my friend comes over and picks me up. I don't really remember why, but it was the night before my folks were leaving.

I go over to his house, and my folks leave, and they lock everything up, and I can't get in, and my keys to my truck are in the house, so I have to have Nick drive me around. So, I'm all bummed, and Nick gets these tickets to this Hey Stroker concert and we go. It's not a big thing, just like two hundred people or something, and we're there, and we're hanging out in this patio thing, and I see Erica, and she's with these people I know.

She comes over and sits down and we're talking, and she asks me to save her seat while she goes and does something. So I do, and she comes back, and we talk, and I really like her. So, she goes to hang with her friends for a bit, and Nick comes over and says we got to go. I'm trying to see Erica, but then I got to go with Nick, so I don't even get to say good-bye to Erica or anything.

The next day, I really want to see her, so I get her pager number from some of the people I know that were hanging with her, and I page her, but I don't hear back. I'm calling again, and find out that she might be at this party. That night, I get Nick and we go to this party, and I see Erica, and she's so into it, that I found her. The next day, we instant message each other, and we want to get together to see the fireworks and everything. It was Fourth of July.

I was so stoked. So I have to get Nick to give me a ride, and by the time I get there, the fireworks are all over, and Erica is kind of bummed, but I stayed, and we really liked being together. That was two years ago, and now we're talking about getting married. It was so messed up to try to find her and get there, with Nick and everything, but she's really changed the way I think about things, and how I am. I mean, I started thinking about her and getting married, and I thought about my folks. They got married when they were really young, like 19 or something. Anyway, I started thinking about that, and I started to kind of see my Dad in a different way, and I didn't want to fight so much. So, Erica's working, and I'm working, and we're both going to community college, and we really love each other's family, and it's so cool.

Kieran—19

So, how do you act to take advantage of a good thing? How do you seize the day, put more money on the table when, in the past, you've been presented with an opportunity and just stood there stammering? Anticipate it! Be prepared. If meeting that girl or guy was something you wanted, *assume* that it will happen at some point and think about what you would say. Rehearse your speech. Anticipate what that person will say. How many times have you been in an argument and thought of the perfect come back an hour later? Could you have anticipated the argument? Could you have been prepared? A perfect example of this is found in job interviews. Have you really thought about what they are going to ask you? One of the first things an interviewer usually asks is for you to tell them about yourself. I was always surprised at how unprepared people are for this question. What are you going to say? You should rehearse this speech and plan it out so that you have a good, one-minute description of yourself, your talents, your accomplishments, your skills, education, and so on.

It's harder to immediately avoid the bad things because I'm not talking about just running away, which never works no matter how hard you try. Go out and find someone who has a Rottweiler. Take the dog off its leash, smack it hard on the head to get its attention, growl at it, show your teeth, and then run from it. When you get out of the emergency room, realize that this is always the result of running away. The problem, issue, or situation will eventually chase you down and maul you. Avoiding a bad thing, putting less money on the table for these losing hands, involves immediately dealing with and getting through the bad thing. You simply have less invested that way, less money on the table. There's a rule in business that your first loss is your best loss. When you are in a losing proposition, accept the loss and get out! In business, trying to save a bad investment is a guaranteed cure for wealth. In life, trying to save a bad situation, trying to make it good, is a guaranteed cure for being lucky.

END THE BAD STUFF QUICKLY

Say you have a book report that is due today. You have typed it up and it is very good work. As you are proudly walking to school, your report in hand, that neighbor's Rottweiler leaps from the bushes, grabs the report from your hand, and reduces it to confetti. This is a bad thing. Say you show up at class and explain this to your teacher, telling him what a great report it was, how much time and effort you put into it. The teacher says "Nice try!" You can argue, you can fight, you can drag this situation out until the end of the semester. You are just investing more time, effort, and energy into a bad thing. Accept your loss, retype the paper, and turn it in the next day. Get over it. Avoid the neighbor's Rottweiler.

Controlling dumb luck, both good and bad, is really just an issue of recognizing it for what it is. If you maximize your bets on the good stuff when you see it's happening and minimize the bad stuff, you have just shifted the odds way in your favor. If you apologized to that girl or guy you bumped into and told them that you had wanted to meet them (honesty and sincerity are very good nunchakus), you may well be on your way to getting to know this person, something you desired to do. Putting in that extra hour to retype your book report and turning it in the next day puts an end, once and for all, to the Rottweiler incident—no more time, effort, or energy is expended on the bad thing. I hope that you can see here how some people end up spending so much time and effort trying to "undo" or "redo" bad stuff, and get so caught up in trying to "fix" things that they then have virtually no time or effort left to take advantage of the good stuff. You control dumb luck by shifting the odds in your favor.

So, what about regular old "luck"? Why does it seem that some people have so many good things happen to them? These people seem to be lucky for two reasons. One reason, whether they are aware of it or not, is that they are maximizing good "dumb luck" and minimizing the bad "dumb luck." If the bumping in the hallway results in ten hours spent with this person you wanted to meet, and the Rottweiler incident results in one hour of retyping the report, it will seem that this person is ten times as lucky as they are unlucky! The other reason people are lucky is that, regardless of whether they are aware of it or not, they have learned how to recognize opportunities and, more importantly, make opportunities for themselves. This is totally all about timing.

KNOCK, KNOCK?

Timing is everything because you can be in the right place at the right time if you give it even a little bit of forethought. Any particular thing that you would like to accomplish, no matter how big or how small, will require three things—the *opportunity*, the *skills*, and the *time*. You are in complete control of the skills and the time, and if you start thinking the right way, you can "create" the opportunities.

Let's assume you want to get on the water polo team. The first thing you need to do is think about the opportunity—the skills and the time. Remember the "knowing what you don't know" and "the need for good information" from the previous sections. The "opportunity" here will be the team tryouts. That's how you get on the team. Do you know when that will be? Next, you need to look at the "skills." Do you have the skills? Do you know all the rules to water polo and the various positions? Do you know who else will be trying out? Do you know who else is returning to the team from last year? Do you know how you compare to the other kids who will be trying out? Do you have the time before tryouts to gain the skills you'll need? Ah ha! You are starting to have a plan. You are starting to think. You are starting to make your own luck.

As you start to gather good information (things you don't know), you find out that only three slots are going to really be open on the team, the rest will be filled by kids who were on the team last year. (You could probably find this out from the coach. Plus this is, in itself, a good opportunity to "brown nose" a little, to make yourself known.) It's probably harder to find out who else will be trying out, but you might ask the coach what positions the returning kids play. You might find out that the coach is going to be a little weak on defenders. With some time on your hands (between finding out this information and when tryouts are held), you can work on your defending skills. This is all related to the concept of Thinking Forward from the introduction. When the day of the tryouts is upon you, you have done everything you can to be lucky. Of the kids competing for those three slots, the coach already knows you (and probably respects your commitment, information gathering, and seeking him out), and you have hopefully gained enough defender skills to meet a need that he has. There is no guarantee, but you have certainly done your best to stack the odds in your favor. The kids that don't get on the team will probably mope around about how "lucky" you were. You commanded the opportunity, the skills, and the time. You were the master of your destiny. You made your own luck!

CREATE YOUR OPPORTUNITY

You can create opportunities by being clever. Back to the bumping in the hallway. Although not a great example, you could position yourself so that this is likely to happen. Better yet, you could find out some things (more stuff you don't know) and discover that this person you want to meet goes to the gym every Tuesday after school. You could put yourself in a position to "naturally" meet as they come out of the gym at 4:30. It's about finding the right place and the right time, and this is much better than having to tackle the people you want to meet!

You can do this with virtually any situation and the fates will smile down upon you. There's another Fact of Life buried in this example that is really important in making your own luck. This is recognizing the WIIFM principle. This stands for "What's In It For Me?" In almost any situation, in virtually any endeavor you may find yourself, there are usually other people involved. You want something (to be on the water polo team) and other people who can affect this want something too (the coach wants some defenders). By imagining that every person you see has WIIFM tattooed on their forehead, you will get very good at creating your own luck. You will find that people really don't want very much out of life, and if you can demonstrate how you can help them get what *they* want, they will be very happy to help you get what *you* want. This is a huge Fact of Life. You scratch my back, and I'll scratch yours!

Managing your life based on the WIIFM principle will immediately set you free. The world will be your oyster (whatever that means). Imagine that whenever you need anything from anyone, the first thing you will hear from them is, "Yeah, well, what's in it for me?" If you are prepared to answer this question, if you have put a little thought into it, you will be able to present a compelling argument. Most people will not be so blunt and say what's in it for me out loud. It's a *very* courteous gesture to offer the answer to this question without it being asked. Say you need help fixing the alternator on your car. You know a guy who can do the work and this guy needs help getting his computer fixed. You can fix a computer, but you can't fix a car. A proposal is born. Thinking about WIIFM is a great tool and it has a counterintuitive side also.

Because most folks don't have the WIIFM tool in their holster, they will yammer along about something they need from you without providing any well-thought-out reasons why you should go out of your way. You have to ask yourself, "What's in it for me," and think about what *you* can expect to get out of the deal. This will put you well on your way to maximizing your *good* dumb luck and minimizing your *bad* dumb luck. Say a good friend of yours wants you to drive with him to pick up an ounce of pot. Let's say that you don't even smoke pot. *What's in it for you?* This is a favor that your friend might feel obligated to return, but there's a significant chance that there could be trouble with the person selling it or with the police. There could be trouble driving with the pot in the car. Here, the potential bad "what's in it for you" far outweighs the potential good "what's in it for you." Decline this offer!

THE RIGHT PLACE, THE RIGHT TIME

You should also be seeing how this WIIFM principle has to do with being in the right place at the right time, or being in the wrong place at the wrong time. This has to do with another business phrase, "If you want to hunt elephants, you must first go to where the elephants are." This means that if you want a tractor, you will have a much better chance of getting one by going to a place that sells or rents tractors. It also means that if you want trouble, you can go to places where trouble is found. Simply keeping yourself away from these places gives you much better odds of not finding trouble. This is an example of avoiding bad luck.

As you start to think about the right places and the right time, you should begin to start thinking forward in your life. Just like being on the water polo team was centered around the opportunity of the tryouts, certain things in your life will be centered around events that you can anticipate. If you go back to the timelines in Section Two and look at what usually happens to people in the various decades of their lives, you can see what's coming at you, the timing of it all, and be totally prepared. You will appear to be very, very lucky.

In your twenties, you are going to need a job. You are going to have to start earning your own money. This is a Fact of Life. You have time on your hands to get prepared, time to get the skills that will be a lot of help. A college education, a technical skill, and certain training can all make finding the job much easier. Thinking about people who might be able to help you get a job and ingratiating yourself to them (like the water polo coach) is a great idea. These people may be parents of your friends, relatives, or friends of the family. Don't wait until you're desperate to "hit them up." Start "softening them up" now! You will appear to be very lucky, when in truth you are just thinking and being prepared.

In your twenties you will probably get married. Since in most cases you can only marry someone you know, what are you doing to see that you are hanging out with girls who are the "marrying kind"? If you find you're in your mid to late twenties and spending most of your free time in beer bars, are you likely to meet the kind of girl you want to marry? Girls get this much more than guys, so I wrote this from the male perspective. As you start looking forward, knowing deep down in your gut how important it is to be at the right place at the right time, you will find that it's really not that hard to do.

Revenge of the Nerds

My mother is Japanese and my father is American. I look a lot like my Mother, and my brother looks a lot like my Dad. We don't really look like we're all one family when we go out, but this is not what my story is about.

Every summer, for as long as I can remember, we have taken a trip to Japan to visit my Mom's family there. The last couple of years, it's been just my Mom and I, as my Dad has been busy, and although my brother speaks Japanese better than I do, he doesn't really like to go anymore because he says the locals don't treat him very well. Evidently, when we're in the town that my Grandparents live in, the other kids our age are pretty mean to him because he doesn't look Japanese enough or something. This is not what my story is about either, but it's kind of interesting.

Anyway, for the last couple of years, my mother and I have gone to Japan to visit her parents and her sister. They live in a pretty small town outside of Kyoto. Both Kyoto and the town my grandparents live in are beautiful, and I love the time we spend there. It's especially fun for me because we've been doing this for years, and I've come to have good friends there. Although I'm only there for a month, I've kind of grown up with the kids who live in my grandparent's neighborhood, and since I look very Japanese, I don't have any trouble like my brother did. It might be because I'm a girl, and boys are more competitive. My friends make fun of my accent, but it's in a nice way, kind of like if you have a relative from the South or something.

Although anyone at home would say I speak fluent Japanese, when I'm there, I can tell that I don't. I'm always using old slang, things kids said on my last trip, or trying to express a feeling that I have, and not being able to find the right words. My friends there love to hear about my life at home, what's going on in our school, what everybody is wearing or listening to. I guess, typical girl stuff, and this is what my story is about.

There's a girl there who lives just a couple of houses down from my grandparent's house. Her name is Keiko. She is beautiful and very good at sports, but not very good at school. On my last trip, I found out that the other girls are not very friendly with Keiko anymore, and the reason is something that no one at home would understand. The reason they don't like Keiko anymore is because she gets poor grades in school. At home, a very pretty and athletic girl like Keiko would be so popular! She'd be even more popular because she didn't really care about her grades. She'd be so cool. In fact, most of the most popular girls in my school at home are exactly like Keiko. They care a lot about how they look, and care very little about how they do in school. In Japan, it's just the opposite. Don't get me wrong, everybody likes pretty girls, but in Japan there is so much emphasis on doing well. It's like "revenge of the nerds"—the thing really respected is performance and not how cool everybody is. This is a huge difference in my two cultures, and I think the Japanese have got it right. They can get a little carried away with it, but it makes everyone really think about who they are and how hard they are working instead of what they're wearing, how they look, or who they hang out with.

I think this is a big reason there is much less trouble for kids in Japan. They have different kinds of trouble, and some kids just have troubled lives anyway, but there is much, much less drug or alcohol use, I've never heard of anyone running away, and generally, the kids I know get along much better with their parents. I know this may sound kind of "nerdy" of me, but at least the kids I know there seem to be a whole lot happier with their lives than my friends at home. I think that learning to concentrate on the really important stuff makes it easier to be much more in touch with yourself, and happier with your place in the world.

Nikki – 16

AN…TISSS…AH…PATION!

Epictetus said it so simply and so clear two thousand years ago: "Seek out the things you desire, and avoid that which you detest." Anticipate that as you grow older you will face different obstacles in life, and that you (being older) will be a different person facing them. What you desire and what you may wish to avoid will change. Stop thinking in such a short-term manner. Look at The Big Picture. An interesting way to think about this is the parable of the Moth and Winter.

A moth has a life span of only three months. Say a particular moth emerges from its cocoon in September. The moth goes about its business, doing whatever moths do, throughout the fall season. The weather is relatively nice, maybe a little windy, and somewhat of a chill is in the air, but all in all, it's pretty pleasant. As the moth reaches old age (November) things will be getting colder and colder, and there might even be a bit of snow. Our fictional moth will think back over the history of its entire life and not have any experience with which to prepare for winter. Fortunately, we are not moths, and we have the ability to gain from experience that is not our own (by reading, talking to people, and asking for advice). We have no reason not to be ready for winter, yet generation after generation of kids enter early adulthood like a deer in headlights. How stupid can we be?

As a teenager, nothing in your meager experience is really going to prepare you for being on your own (winter). Being on your own and supporting yourself (and perhaps others) is nothing like being an infant. It is nothing like being a child. It is nothing like being an adolescent or a teen. You have no direct experience with which to meet the impending challenges of life. You have to be smarter than the moth. You have to realize what's coming at you ("Is that the light at the end of the tunnel, or an oncoming train?"). You have to take the time you have and make sure you get the skills you are going to need so that when you arrange an opportunity, you will be able to succeed. If you do nothing more than these things, you will find that you will be considered one of the "luckiest" people around. Why wouldn't you want to have a great job, a successful spouse, wonderful children of your own? It's all there for the taking, and the folks that are doing the most thinking about their lives are the ones who get to take the most out of it! You might as well be one of them!

* * *

Key Points

So you've got all the luck stuff. You really see how luck can make up for a whole lot of shortcomings. Being lucky is as easy as being in the right place at the right time, while being unlucky is simply a matter of being in the wrong place at the wrong time. Understand that you have equal odds of *good* dumb luck and *bad* dumb luck happening to you. Those people who are able to put more money on the table for the good stuff, seize the day, and take advantage of opportunities will appear to be very, very lucky! Avoid the bad dumb luck by investing the least amount of time, energy, and effort into it. Be done with it. Never run away—shift the odds in your favor and make opportunities. Be ready for potential conversations! Think about your goals in terms of opportunity, skills, and time. Make sure you have all three! Do all this stuff and you will start making your own luck.

Start thinking about the WIIFM of the people you have to deal with, and you not only be lucky—you will be a very popular individual. Never forget the WIIFM "flip side" by knowing what is in something for *you*! Look forward, plan forward, and think forward. Use your small planning skills (the water polo team) on the big stuff you know is coming up. Make your small planning work big. Pay attention to what you are seeking and what you wish to avoid. Don't be stupid. Don't be a moth fluttering around in the snowfall!

✳ ✳ ✳

You should now spend a little time talking about this:

- Can you name some "right place, right time" situations and some "wrong" ones?
- Do you understand how to put more or less money on the table in life?
- Name a situation where you ran away. Did it catch up?
- What's an opportunity you would like to make?
- Can you describe how opportunity, time, and skill work together?
- Do you get the WIIFM principle?
- Do you get the "flip side" of the WIIFM principle?
- Can you name a small plan you would like to start working on?
- What's the first big plan you would like to start working on?

ABOUT THE AUTHOR

Bill Bernard has had a twenty-five year career as a successful media executive, most recently creating and running a cable-television shopping network. He is a frequent speaker at conferences and conventions. Bernard has also raised five teenagers in a blended household. He lives in San Clemente, California.